Edith Œnone Somerville (1858–1 _____ County Cork, Ireland. She belonge _____ Anglo-Irish society, and appropria _____ particularly its cult of fox-hunting, ___ ___ _____ ____ always towards the arts. After a private education at home she studied art in Düsseldorf, Paris and London, and began her career as an illustrator. Though, after her meeting with her cousin, Violet Martin, in 1886, and the beginning of their long collaboration, she was best known as a writer.

Martin Ross (1862–1915) was born at Ross House, County Galway, Ireland. She took her pseudonym, 'Ross' from her native place. She was educated first by governesses at home, and then at Alexandra College, Dublin. She was an ardent suffragist, and was vice-president of the Munster Women's Franchise League. In 1898, Violet Martin was severely injured in a riding accident, which resulted in several years of invalidism, and which may have contributed to her early death.

Somerville and Ross lived together for most of their lives at the Somerville home in County Cork. They travelled a great deal together in Europe, and spent months at a time in Paris. Separately and together, they wrote some thirty books, mainly set in Ireland, as well as many articles, letters, diaries and jottings. Their first collaboration was *An Irish Cousin* (1889) followed by *Through Connemara in a Governess Cart* (1893), also published by Virago, a commission from the *Ladies' Pictorial* to do a series of travel articles which would later make up a book. Among their many collaborations, *The Real Charlotte* (1894, televised for ITV in 1991) was their first serious novel and generally conceded to be their best. Their most popular books, however, were the rollicking *Some Experiences of the Irish R.M.* (1899) and *Further Experiences of the Irish R.M.* (1908), which had a success they were never able to duplicate.

When Martin Ross died, Edith Œ. Somerville, deeply affected by her cousin's death, said: 'I have known her help and have thankfully received her inspiration. She has gone, but our collaboration is not ended.' She wrote another thirteen books under the name of 'Somerville and Ross'.

E. Œ. SOMERVILLE
& MARTIN ROSS

....

IN THE VINE COUNTRY

ILLUSTRATED BY F. H. TOWNSEND
FROM SKETCHES BY EDITH Œ. SOMERVILLE

Published by VIRAGO PRESS Limited 1991
20-23 Mandela Street, Camden Town, London NW1 0HQ

First published by W. H. Allen & Co. Limited 1893
Virago Press edition reproduced from the W. H. Allen & Co.
first edition

*A CIP catalogue record for this book is available from the
British Library*

Printed in Great Britain by Cox and Wyman Ltd., Reading, Berks

The following pages, with their accompanying Illustrations, originally appeared in the columns of 'The Lady's Pictorial,' and are here reprinted by permission of the Proprietors.

IN THE VINE COUNTRY.

CHAPTER I.

T was our first day's cub-hunting, and
things had been going against us from
the outset.

To begin with, we had started rather late,—it is
noticeable that the minutes between five and six
A.M. are fewer and closer together than they are at
any other period of the day,—and, when half way to
the meet we found that Betty had given way to her
sporting proclivities, and had surreptitiously followed
us. When it is explained that Betty is a St. Bernard
puppy of cart-horse dimensions, whose expression of
smiling imbecility only cloaks a will of iron, it will
be understood that there was trouble before us. The

7

trouble began at once.　Directly she saw she was discovered she ran away, and the next time we saw her
she was three fields ahead of us, lumbering cheerfully
into covert at the heels of the hounds, pursued by
several cows and the curses of the master.

BETTY.

By the time that she had been caught and immured
in the bedroom of the nearest cottage, we were
covered with confusion and blazing with heat, and
while we were precariously scrambling on to our
horses' backs by the help of the pigstye door, we were

told by an excited old man that the hounds had found, and were 'firing away like the divil' out of the far side of the wood. This happened to be one of those statements that are founded not so much on fact as on a desire to keep things stirring and pleasant, but none the less did it send us at inconvenient speed to the other side of the covert, there to find that the hounds had never left it, and were hunting slowly back towards the side from which we had just come.

Not long after this my second cousin lost her temper, and said she hated cubbing, and wished she was back in Connemara, or anywhere out of the county Cork. This expression of opinion occurred when she was picking herself up out of a potato furrow, into which she and her horse had ingloriously rolled, and it was a good deal embittered by the fact that she had hurt her knee, torn her habit, and broken her hunting crop.

The day ended with this incident, so far, at least, as we were concerned. Betty was released from the captivity that she had not ceased to bewail in quivering, infantine shrieks, and we turned our faces toward home.   There is something very humbling in coming in at ten o'clock to a late edition of the family breakfast, with nothing to justify the routing up of the household at five A.M. except a torn habit and a bruised knee ; and we said to each other, as we went unostentatiously up the back stairs, that cubbing was not worth the candle by which one had to get up to be in time for it.

We did not know that a few days afterwards we should be hanging out of the window of the train as, at a painfully early hour, it passed a covert in the vicinity, straining jaundiced eyes of jealousy at the distant specks that represented the field and the hounds—specks who were to remain in the county Cork and go out cubbing, instead of faring forth, as we were doing, to take our pleasure in foreign lands.

The letter that we found on the dining-room table, when we came down-stairs on that day that had

MY SECOND COUSIN LOST HER TEMPER.

been sacrificed to Betty, was responsible for this unexpected change of circumstances. It said majestically, 'You are to go to the vineyards of the Médoc, and must start at once in order to be in time for the vintage;' and in spite of a grand and complete ignorance of Médoc, its vintages, and wines in general, we accepted the position with calm, even with satisfaction.

The gibes of our friends were many and untiring, and were the harder to bear that we felt a secret scepticism as to our fitness for this large and yet delicate mission,—what did we know of Château Lafite or Mouton Rothschild, except that a glass and a half of the former had once compelled my second cousin to untimely slumber at dessert?—and when on a foggy morning we drove away from home, the dank air was heavy with the prognostications that we should return as bottle-nosed dipsomaniacs, and the last thing that caught our eye as we turned the final corner of the avenue was the flutter of a piece of blue ribbon.

We had a singularly detestable journey to London, or perhaps it was that a summer spent in country remoteness made the train and its loathsome sister, the steamboat, more intolerable than usual. As far as Dublin we were comparatively confident, though the trees at the station were rustling a little in the wind, and the window-frames shook ominously in dismal accompaniment to the lamentations of the emigrants who crowded the platforms, waiting for the down train to Cork. There are happily few things in the world that are as bad as they are expected to be, but a bad crossing is worse than the combined efforts of imagination and remembrance can make it. This, at least, is the opinion of my second cousin, who ought by this time to have some knowledge of a subject to which, according to her own reckoning of the time occupied in each crossing, she has given some fifty of the best years of her life. The trees and the window-frames had not overstated the case, and we had the gloomy satisfaction of hearing the stewardess remark, as we neared Holyhead, that it had been a rough passage. We could have told her so ourselves, but still it was gratifying to have the thing placed on an official basis.

In the pale morning, as we endured that last long hour before Euston is reached, we read in headachy snatches a pamphlet that we had been lent about the wines of the Médoc, and our souls sank at the prospect of expounding the laws of fermentation to readers who would be as oppressively bored by it as we ourselves. But our first day in London routed this hobgoblin: we were to enjoy ourselves; we were to taste claret if we wished, or talk bad French to the makers of it if it amused us; but to improve other people's minds by figures and able disquisitions on viticulture and the treatment of the phylloxera was not, we heard with thanksgiving, to be our mission.

The three days before our start were spent in the manner customary in such cases; that is to say, we moved incessantly and at an ever-quickening pace between the Strand, the Army and Navy Stores, and High Street, Kensington, laden with small parcels,

footsore from the unaccustomed flagstones, and care-
worn from the effort to utilise the Underground return
tickets that an ideally perfect programme had induced

WE WERE LENT A KODAK.

us to take in the morning. In addition to these usual
cares, another more poignant anxiety fell to our lot.
We were lent a Kodak,—for the benefit of the

unlearned it may be mentioned that the Kodak is a photographic camera of the kind that is to the ordinary species as a compressed meat lozenge to a round of beef,—and as neither of us knew anything about it, it became necessary to learn its mechanism in a fevered ten minutes, or to leave it behind. Ambition fired us to the attempt, and having adjourned with the Kodak and an instructor to the severely simple scenery of the gardens on the Thames Embankment, we received there our first and only lesson. What its results were will never be known to the public; a group of intoxicated ghosts lolling on a bench in the depths of a spotted fog can be of little interest to any one except the artists, and even to their indulgent eyes its charm is of a somewhat morbid character.

After these agitations, the corner seats of a railway carriage at Victoria had a restful luxury about them that. was almost stagnation. The consciousness of two portmanteaus registered to Bordeaux almost made up for the cumbrous row of hand packages that

2

squatted in the netting; and the half-hour of waiting
for the train to start was a period of soothing inaction
scarcely ruffled by the slow filling of the carriage to
its limit of five on each side, and merely moved to a
languid enjoyment by the inexorable determination
of the latest comers, a bride and bridegroom, to sit
next to each other irrespective of all previous arrangements of old ladies and their baskets. They had
about them the well-known power of making their
innocent and well-meaning fellow-creatures feel in the
way and in the wrong, and the eyes of the carriage
sought the windows or the ceiling as if by word of
command when, after the settling down of glowingly
new bags and rugs was completed, the latest comers
leaned back and gazed into each other's faces with an
unaffected ecstasy, the fact that both wore gold-
rimmed spectacles imparting a sort of serious lustre
to their mutual regard. The gaze seemed to us to
last most of the way to Dover, except at those
moments when a glance or two was given to their
fellow-passengers, a glance of almost compassionate

wonder that people so uninteresting and so superfluous should be alive. It gave us an instant of pleasure when some time afterwards on board the boat we saw that the bride's fringe was blown into dejected wisps, and that her groom's nose was blue and his face pinched.

Before we reached Dover an example was vouchsafed to us in further proof, if such were needed, of the difficulty of saying good-bye agreeably at the window of a railway carriage. In this case the victims of the custom stood on the platform, smiling spasmodically at the other victim in the carriage, and saying at intervals, 'Well, you'll write, won't you?' 'So good of you to come and see me off.' 'Well, *mind* you write!' 'Oh yes, dear, and be sure you give my love to Mary and Aunt Williams.' Then they all smiled brightly and nodded their heads, and the traveller, with her chin upon the window-sill, beamed galvanically down upon her friends, and in her turn adjured them not to forget to write. As the train moved off at last, the farewells thickened to a climax,

and we were privileged to observe how, when the final
delicate flutter of the hand had been given, the smile
disappeared from the face of the traveller, and she
thankfully yielded herself to the deferred enjoyment
of her newspaper.

Of the further journey to Paris there is happily
little to record. '*Das höchste Glück hat reine Lieder,*'
and the most satisfactory travelling is that which
lends itself least to description. The Calais boat
made its journey in the most brilliant of sunshine
and the most refreshing of breezes, trampling its way
along the water at a pace that made the tall merchant-
men look more old-world and stately than usual as
they moved serenely down the Channel. The male
part of the passengers walked the deck as if their lives
depended on it, after the custom of men ; the ladies
sat in sheltered places and tried to keep their hair
tidy ; and all alike exhibited the hypnotic consciousness of the presence of a sketch-book, that makes the
most cautious sketcher the object of instant remark
and suspicion.

We sat that night in the warm, airless courtyard of
a Paris hotel ; tall dusty shrubs in pots hung their
lank leaves limply over our heads ; waiters flitted like
bats to and fro between the kitchen on one side and
the *salle-à-manger* on the other. A French family,
consisting of a papa, a mamma, a beautifully behaved
daughter with her hair in a queue, a humorous old
friend of a godfatherly type, and a little boy with
tasselled boots, partook of various liquids at a table
near enough to us to permit of our hearing their
effortless, endless babble, and also to observe with
ever-growing hatred the self-conscious gambols of
the little boy. Later on, they adjourned to the *salon*,
and the daughter performed a selection of music.
She began with a confident rendering of '*La Prière
d'une Vierge*,' one of those pieces which once was the
strength and glory of every budding pianiste, but now
in its old age is only heard limping and faltering over
the greasy keys of hotel pianos ; and she finished
with an operatic gallop in which the treble fled about
in lonely frenzy, and the bass retired on to the lowest

octave of the piano and there had a fit of St. Vitus's dance. The little boy pirouetted about the room, the papa, mamma, and godfather clapped their hands and laughed indulgently, and a good many of the windows that gave on to the courtyard were suddenly and violently shut.

We went to bed after that ; that is to say, we retired into a good-sized opera-box, with windows opening on to lamps and palms, and a general interior effect of red curtains and mirrors. It is one of the strangest features of French hotels that dressing-tables are not included in any suite of bedroom furniture ; there are looking-glasses by the score, there are handsome marble slabs bearing ornate clocks that do not go, there are gorgeous *armoires à glace*, but never a good, commonplace, useful dressing-table. French people seem to do without them in the same simple, uncomplaining way that they do without baths.

We cannot pretend to say we slept well in our opera-box. Everything in the hotel seemed to stay up

all night, including a small but devoted party of fleas ;
and the atmosphere, even when diluted with as much

HE BROKE INTO A DEFIANT POLKA.

courtyard air as the windows would let in, was heavy

and hot. We came down next morning feeling un-
refreshed, and not at all disposed to bestow of our
substance on the street musician who, since eight
o'clock, had been playing national airs on an
accordion in the courtyard. Having seen us pass by
on our way to breakfast, he immediately played
'God save the Queen,' gliding subsequently into the
'Marseillaise' as a kind of corrective, and then finding that we still drank our coffee unmoved, he broke
into a defiant polka, which, did he but know it, has
'sung in our sleeping ear and hummed in our waking
head' in elusive, half-remembered snatches, revenging
a thousandfold the callousness of the two *Anglaises*.

We had not much time to spare after breakfast, as
the Bordeaux train by which we were going started
at 11.20. A mosquito net was, however, one of the
things we had forgotten, and one of the things which
we were assured was indispensable, and it was not
until we had entered a likely-looking shop that we
realised that we did not know the French for
mosquito. My second cousin and the shopwoman

regarded each other for a few seconds in polite
silence, and then the latter said interrogatively,—

‘ *Madame désire— ?* ’

RESOLVED THAT DEATH ALONE SHOULD PART US FROM BELLOWS’
DICTIONARY.

My second cousin answered diffidently that she
desired fine net as a—as a—in short, for a veil against
the—the flies that bite.

The shopwoman looked at her with compassion, and offered me a handsome long black lace veil, and with it the assurance that mademoiselle would find it very becoming. At this stage in the negotiation the two purchasers began to laugh with the agonising laughter that has too often overtaken them in shops, and the shopwoman, as is usual in such cases, was obviously convinced that she was being laughed at, and haughtily replaced the lace veil in its box. Having wept profusely and idiotically before her for some moments, we recovered sufficiently to ask for white muslin, and succeeded in buying a suitable piece, with which we slunk out of the shop, resolved that in future death alone should part us from Bellows' Dictionary.

CHAPTER II.

'TWENTY minutes—half an hour — three-quarters — what mademoiselle pleases!'

This was what the waiter said when we asked him how long it would take to drive to the Gare d'Orléans on the morning that we left Paris. We selected half an hour, and by so doing as nearly as possible missed our train— in fact, when we arrived at the Quai d'Austerlitz the station clock was already at the hour of departure. It was consoling to be told officially that it was five minutes fast, but five minutes does not go far in the maddening routine

of French stations, and we were wrecks, mentally
and physically, by the time we had wedged ourselves
into the crowded carriage, labelled 'Bordeaux—
Bastide,' that was to be our portion. French railway
officials never weary of this little practical joke of
·keeping the outside clock of the station five minutes
fast. If they did it always it would lose its piquancy,
but they guard against this by occasional deviations
into truth, so that the nerve of the public is
effectively shattered, and the station officials never
fail of amusement.

Eleven hours in a train is an immeasurable time,
especially when the train goes through a country
that, after a first hour or so of picturesqueness, lacks
absolutely any distinction of colour or outline.
Greyish tilled plains stretched away on either side,
without a fence, without a boundary, except for the
occasional rows of housemaids' mops and birch-rods
that enlivened the horizon. These detachments of
poplars are inseparable from French travelling; they
haunt the ridges of the plains like the ghosts of

worthier trees, with all the dejection befitting those who know that they are only worth a few francs, and can hope for no better transmigration than a kitchen table or a pig's trough. The country seemed silent and empty after the harvest ; we saw very few living things except flocks of sheep, and we meditated with an ever-growing wonder on what might be the moral suasion that kept each of these on its own undefended square of grass. Arguing from the more than demoniacal perverseness of Irish sheep in breaking bounds, it seemed to us that the French must have hit on the supreme expedient of offering no resistance whatever, and thereby destroyed at one blow the essential joy of trespass.

The train progressed in an easy canter, giving us time to observe all wayside objects : we could have counted the big *citrouilles* that lay in magnificent obesity, with their sunset-hued cheeks glowing like fire on the colourless fields, suggestive of immeasurable pumpkin squash, and we could see on the low bushes that we had at first taken for currant trees,

the black clusters that told we had at last come into
the wine country. It was not so pleasant to see in
the waiting-room at Poitiers the black clusters of
men, each enveloped in his own halo of garlic or bad
tobacco smoke, that told us our chance of getting a
cup of coffee was not worth the attendant horror of
elbowing our way through them to the buffet. We
had not got over the strangeness of knowing that at
any or every small hotel or railway station we could
have a really good cup of coffee, unflavoured by
chicory, liquorice, blackbeetles, or whatever may be
the master ingredient in the muddy draught that
is invariable at such places in England, and we had
looked forward to Poitiers with an enthusiasm quite
unconnected with the Black Prince, or any other
romantic memory of Mrs. Markham's *History of
England.*

By the time we reached Angoulême it was quite
dark, and we had fallen into the sodden stupefaction
of travel. The carriage was nearly empty, and the
lamp cast a distorted light upon the puckered faces

of the old lady and gentleman who were our only
fellow-travellers, as their heads nodded and rolled
in anxious, uneasy slumber. The small stations
became more frequent, and we were drearily aware
of the same routine at each : the half-dozen lights of
a village across the fields, the nasal bellow of an
unintelligible name, the thump of a box or two on
the platform, and finally a sound that we took at
first for the bleat of a tethered kid, but which we
discovered to be the note of a small trumpet or horn,
wound by the guard as the signal for departure.
It was only towards the end of the journey that this
implement had replaced the ordinary whistle, and
for about eight or ten stations we laughed at it ;
after that the lament of the kid added itself seriously
to the general gloom.

The last hour or two before Bordeaux would have
been much harder to bear but for a display of sheet
lightning, the like of which we had never seen
before. The sudden beautiful flicker played hide-
and-seek like a living creature among the curtains of

cloud, flashing about all the points of the compass
between south and east, or sometimes thrusting to
and fro across an opening, like glimpses of the
rapiers in a giants' fencing bout. It was under this
mocking, elfish light that we first sighted Bordeaux
and its river, and realised that the time had come
for us to strap up our rugs, and say 'pardon' in our
best French accent to the old gentleman on whose
feet we trod as we did so, and to drag our stiff
bodies forth into the electric glare of the station.
We had reached such a stage of fatigue and
demoralisation that we should rather have stayed in
the carriage all night, and gone on with the old
lady to a place she called 'Erin,' in a fine Hammer-
smith twang. We should not have cared much
whether it proved to be the land of our birth, or
Irun, on the Spanish frontier, which we now believe
to have been her destination.

We had a long quarter of an hour to wait before
the *Douane* could bring itself to give up its dead,
and there was another quarter of an hour of driving

through deserted and badly-lighted streets before we got to our hotel. We crossed a bridge that must have been half a mile long, we feigned to each other an interest in a half-seen gateway at the end of it, and our hearts were all the time groping in a certain hold-all, where lay a spirit-kettle, a teapot, and half a pound of English tea. The offensively urbane and wide-awake head waiter, with his clean-shaven face and foxy eyes, had some evident difficulty in repressing his scorn when he heard that he was to *faire monter* to our room a little milk and hot water, but it mounted to our third floor for all that. It was a blow to find a skin on the top of the milk that showed it had once been boiled : we did not know then that French hotels considered milk in its raw, uncooked state to be as baneful as if it were water.

Our room was large, and of a somewhat gloomy magnificence, with towering bed canopies, and darkly-gleaming mahogany ; and as our one *bougie* —valued in the bill at a franc—contended with its surroundings, we felt like a chapter out of almost any of Scott's novels—the chapter where the hero spends a night in some one's private and luxurious dungeon, and having obtained writing materials, has heard the last retreating footsteps of an attendant who has unostentatiously locked and double-locked the door.   What we heard principally, while we drank our surreptitious midnight cup of tea, was not the howling of the storm or the hoarse baying of a bloodhound in the courtyard, but the snoring of some one in the next room.   It was hard to believe that the artist was not doing it on purpose ; each snore was so painstaking, so measured, and had such a careful crescendo in its vibrating fortissimo. He had certainly brought the accomplishment to a high degree of perfection, and if he does not die of concussion of the brain in the attempt, he ought, with a little more practice, to be able to empty any hotel in a single night.

It was broad summer in Bordeaux, so we dis-covered next morning when we escaped from the

OUR SURREPTITIOUS MIDNIGHT CUP OF TEA.

half-light of the coffee-room and walked forth to see the town. We went down to the quays and crawled along them in the shade, looking at the immense river, and the long 'winter woodland' of masts of all countries, stretching away seemingly to the Bay of Biscay: it did not matter that the water was the colour of *café au lait*, churned to dirty froth by innumerable screws and paddles, or that the hoarse screams of steam whistles ascended through black smoke to the brilliant heavens; all was new and delightful, and of a cheerfulness unknown to the British Isles. It was here that we began to realise what the wine country could do when it gave its mind to it. The great quays were packed close with barrels as far as the eye could follow—barrels on whose ends were hieroglyphs that told of aristocratic birth as plainly as the armorial bearings on a carriage; the streets were full of long narrow carts like ladders on wheels, laden also with barrels, one behind the other; and about every five minutes, as it seemed to us, some big ship moved out from the

wharf, filled to the brim with claret, and slipped
down the yellow current to other climes.   As we sat
under the chestnut trees and watched the tide of the
traffic, we began to notice that there are more grey
horses in France than one would have imagined
there could have been in the world.   The streets of
Paris are mottled by them ; the streets of Bordeaux
are mottled in the opposite way—that is to say, the
dark horses are like specks among the white, and in
the Médoc the necessary difficulty of providing black
horses for funerals can probably be only solved by
blacklead.

We carried a map of Bordeaux in our hands, and
stopped many times to study it as we strolled along,
causing thereby an ecstasy of interest among the
sailors and the women sitting at their stalls of
strange fruits and fungi.   It was disappointing that
French wit did not on these occasions elaborate any
jest more sparkling than '*Ah! Les Anglaises!*'
though the inhabitants seemed to find the humour of
the situation satiatingly expressed in this simple

formula. Once, in Paris, a butcher's boy screamed 'Angleesh spock-en' after us, and convulsed the whole street with the sally; but we thought that we could have produced something better any day on Patrick's Bridge, Cork. We perseveringly ciphered out our route to the church of St. Michel, assisted a good deal, it must be admitted, by the fact that its steeple is the tallest thing in Bordeaux. We were getting very hot indeed as we toiled through the Tour de Cailhau—so hot that, as a Galway woman once remarked, 'it would have been a pleasure to any one to lie down and die,' and we longed to sit down and rest on the kerbstone in the shade of the Tour beside a man in a blue blouse who was sharpening a razor in his entirely filthy palm.

This being out of the question, we struggled on towards St. Michel, promising ourselves a bath of coolness and darkness under its lofty roof, and more especially in its underground caverns, where inhabit the celebrated mummies that have been preserved by the soil of the graveyard from dissolution. We

crossed the last and sunniest street, and passed
through a swing door into a large church, consider-
ably hotter than anything or anywhere outside, and
with an atmosphere of an unknown and stifling kind.
We walked round it in silence, and, looking at each
other, as we fanned ourselves with guide-books, we
felt that our last chance of averting heat-apoplexy
was to go underground at once and see the mummies.

We found that the mummies lived in a place apart
from the church, under the *clocher*, as the beautiful
spire is called, by which we had steered our way, and
we approached with feelings of unmitigated awe and
creepiness the doorway to which we had been directed
by two little boys who were playing cards in the
shadow of a buttress. The door itself was round
another buttress, in a low and crumbling stone archway, and we knocked timidly at it. It opened, and
in a room of about the size and shape of a bonnet-
box we beheld, instead of mummies, a cheerful family
party at breakfast. We were about to retire, but the
mother, wiping the *vin ordinaire* from her jovial

mouth, assured us that she was ready to show us the Cellar of the Mummies immediately. We squeezed past the rest of the family, and saw that at their very feet a precipitous stone staircase plunged into darkness.

Our guide picked up a candlestick of a pattern that we were destined to see more of afterwards,—*i.e.* a long piece of wood with a tallow *bougie* erect at one end of it,—and after an anxious inquiry on our parts as to whether there was any scent *là-bas* in the cave had been answered in the negative, we followed her into the abyss. It proved to be a circular vault, made, like everything else in Bordeaux, of dusty yellow stone, and, after a minute of despondency on the part of the *bougie*, we saw, lining its walls, a dismal array of little brown figures, propped on end behind a low wooden rail.

The guide advanced with alacrity to her task.

'Behold, mesdames, the celebrated mummies of St. Michel'—

She paused, and flourished the candle in the awful

faces of a group of objects who were just preserved

'BEHOLD, MESDAMES, THE CELEBRATED MUMMIES OF ST. MICHEL.'

from being skeletons by a ragged covering of dusty
leather which had once been flesh.

' *Voiçi la famille empoisonnée!*   Observe the morsel
still in the mouth of the little one!   Mosh-rhume!
Hein?'   She made a light-hearted attempt at the
English word, but seeing we looked bewildered,
passed easily back into French.   'Mushrooms,
mesdames.   All the family are found dead together!'

We looked at them, but not too closely, and also
at their companions—the porter, the fat woman (now
a shrivelled and dreadful dwarf), the boy who had
been buried alive,—at least, the guide hopefully said
that she was almost sure that he had been buried
alive,—and the General, evidently a special favourite,
who had been frequently wounded in the battle, so
she told us, as an apology for the fact that there was
very little of him left.   How she knew these grue-
some histories we did not inquire, and with the best
intentions in the world we could not altogether
believe them.   There was nothing human or appeal-
ing in these grotesque survivals of three centuries
ago ; they might have been little damaged terra-cotta
figures, had it not been for the dusty grins that

showed unmistakable teeth, and some indefinable sentiment of genuineness and absence of effort.

As we climbed up the stone stairs into the sun and heat, we felt that the immortality thrust upon the mummies of St. Michel was a cruel one; and nothing but the affectionate satisfaction of the able show-woman with her show reconciles us to its memory.

CHAPTER III.

HE steamer that plies between Bordeaux
and Royan, calling *en route* at several
dozen places on the Garonne and Gironde,
is of an unfortunate popularity. From reasons here-
after to be explained, we arrived early at the landing-
stage, and we found the forepart of the vessel already
crammed with blue-clad peasants, from whom, as
they screamed, gesticulated, and even danced in the
ardour of conversation, the well-known odour of
garlic was slowly winnowed forth, and floated aft to
where the first-class passengers sat on rows of cane
chairs under an awning, looking daggers at all new-
comers. We took two seats in the background,
conscious that our English costume was the subject
of a scarcely concealed surprise, and feeling that

neither we nor it were able to bear up against criticism.

We had been much weakened by our last half-hour at the hotel. It is not so much the bill, 'though that,' as Mrs. Browning remarks, 'may be owed,' that whittles the traveller down ; it was not in our case even the *bougie* at a franc,—we had hidden away that *bougie* in our portmanteau, and felt better for it,—it was the hall of the hotel with its feudal band of retainers that had slowly and agonisingly taken from us our presence of mind, our dignity, and lastly our truthfulness. We had tipped our own special waiter, the chambermaid, the boots, and the luggage porter, and seeing dizzily that there were still before us the lusciously smiling and relentless faces of an assistant chambermaid, a deputy-assistant porter, and the head waiter, we said we were going round for a moment to the Bureau of Change, and slid from the hotel with something of the modest self-consciousness of a dog leaving the kitchen with a leg of mutton in its mouth.

It gave us a great deal of trouble to make our way down to the quays without passing the hotel again; but we did it, and enjoyed the slums and the smells as we realised something of what might be the

WE SAID WE WERE GOING ROUND FOR A MOMENT TO THE
BUREAU OF CHANGE.

expressions, facial and otherwise, of the waiter, the porter, and the chambermaid, whom we had left hopefully waiting at the door. Our luggage had been sent on to the boat some time before; that was the fact that had added swiftness and perfectness to our escape, and when, in walking down the long gangway, we saw a boy in *sabots* cutting ungainly capers all the way in front of us, out of the gaiety of his heart, we were grateful to him; he expressed our feelings in a manner denied to us by circumstance.

There was something Irish and homelike about the conduct of our Pauillac steamer in the matter of starting. It was ten minutes after the appointed time when we moved out into the river amongst the big ships that were coming up on the tide, and the little black ferry-boats that flew to and fro like incensed water-spiders, but this was only what might have been expected. What did seem a little hard to bear was, that when we were well out into mid-stream we should put back again to the quay, and embark a fresh cargo of passengers, who had been there from the beginning, apparently trying to make up their minds about whether they would go or not. It was merely a coquettish ruse on the part of the captain to make a pretended start; but it had the desired effect, and when we did get off, every man of the malingerers was safely stacked on the forward deck.

The tide was running up hard, fighting every inch of the way with the strong current of the river, and getting the best of it. It was a singularly dirty strife, involving, like an Irish election, much stirring up of the mud: a conflict in *café au lait*, with a sprinkling of cinders strewed on the top, is not romantic either in colour or suggestion; but by dint of sunshine and strong blue sky, and the seeing it for the first time, there was a kind of furious beauty in the great stretch of river ahead of us, with its yellow waves leaping and wrestling out to the horizon. Bordeaux began to lessen down to a photographic view of itself; the immense bridge and its arches dwindled to a long caterpillar, crawling many-legged across the stream; the thousand delicate details of masts and yards melted into a cobwebby mist, and, behind all, the *clocher* of St. Michel towered above the blur of houses, a monument altogether too magnificent for the deplorable little tribe of mummies that we had that morning viewed in its foundations.

The first-class passengers maintained their attitude of suspicion as far as we were concerned; and when,

AN INTERMITTENT PROCESSION OF MEN.

after a period of discreet inoffensiveness, a sketch-book was called into requisition, they began to be quite sure that we were as objectionable as our clothing, and discussed us in groups, with such lightning side-glances as only French eyes can give. For a little time an intermittent procession of men strolled in an elaborately casual manner round behind the sketch-book ; but, finding themselves rewarded only by Arcadian glimpses of cattle, trees, and churches, they gradually settled down on their chairs again, and smoked the mysterious compound known to the French middle-classes as tobacco, while the cattle and the churches retired into the desert places of the sketch-book, and the page with the fat *curé*, his still fatter friend, and the insatiably curious little boy, came to light again.

For the first half of the journey the steamer made her way down the river on the principle of Billy Malowny's exit from the wake, when 'it wasn't so much the length of the road come agin him as the breadth.' Every house on each bank seemed to have a landing-place of its own, and a passenger to be landed at it ; we crossed and recrossed, as if we were beating to windward, and the Bordeaux merchants and bank clerks returned by scores to the bosoms

of their families, and were no doubt epigrammatic at
dinner on the subject of the two absurdly emanci-
pated *Anglaises*, with their sailor hats and brown
shoes.   At all events, we were getting our first
impressions of the Médoc slowly and thoroughly.
We were in the thick of the Vine Country by this
time ; everywhere, as far as we could see, the low
slopes were seamed and striped with vines till they
looked like green corduroy, and every large house
among them was a *château*, with a name more or
less familiar even to the ignorant and unlearned.
We had a map of the Médoc with us—a map that
gave all the *châteaux* in heavy capitals, and added
the towns as trivial necessities in diamond type ; it
sometimes even gave a little picture of a particularly
pet *château*, so that there might be no mistake about
it.   From this we identified the Château Margaux,
the home of one of the four kings of the classified
Médoc wines, sharing its select first-class with Lafite,
Latour, and Haut-Brion, behind whom trails the
sacred list of the classified, down to the fifth estate,

and after that the deluge of the *bourgeois* wines, most of which are good enough for any one, but are not quite of the blood royal.

It is difficult to realise in the Médoc that the best wine in the world is made in places where there is no tall chimney or hideous range of manufactories. All that one sees is a two-storey country-house, with pointed towers at each end, standing in green vineyard slopes, with somewhere in the background a group of inoffensive and often picturesque houses, painted pink, or some other frivolous colour, and not taking up as much room as the stables and yards at big houses in England. It is the extraordinary independence of grapes that gives this simplicity in wine-making. They do the whole thing themselves, only demanding to be let alone; and not all the tall chimneys in England could coerce them into fermenting a day faster than they choose, or could give them any better flavour than their own laws decree.

We had only one specimen of what is commonly

felt to be landscape, and is spoken of as scenery, as opposed to mere contour, on our way to Pauillac. It was at a place on the right bank of the river, where the shore suddenly reared itself into cliffs of a sunny fawn colour, and apparently of a texture that was eminently suited for house building; so supremely, in fact, that the people of the place had not troubled themselves to cart it away, but had come, like Mohammed, to the mountain, and had blasted themselves out houses in it, and apparently finished them off with their penknives, or teaspoons, or any other implement that was convenient. Some people decorated the front of their cliff very handsomely with carved balustrades and porches; others merely tidied down the rock a little round the windows, and helped out the angles here and there, and put chimneys on handy protuberances. It must have its points as a system of living; when, for instance, the house is crowded for a wedding or a dance, they can dig out a few more spare rooms towards the front, and throw the stuff out of the windows. The rock cuts as easily as wood, and becomes perfectly hard in the air; it is absolutely ideal in all useful respects, and in colour is beautiful, so cheerful and so tempered. We saw these tawny cliffs behind us for a long time, while the boat made her way into the broader flood of the Gironde. The sun made much of them as it sank, and their warm, friendly faces looked still after us in the twilight, when the west was glowing darkly, and the cold wind was forcing us to tramp to and fro in the short span of the deck till we were giddy.

It was past seven o'clock when the lights of Pauillac sparkled ahead of us on the river bank, and we thankfully gathered together our baggage, suborned our sailor, and desired him to lead us to the Grand Hôtel, the one to which we had been recommended. It was a good deal of a shock when he told us that the Grand Hôtel had been closed for a year on account of the death of the proprietor. It was not the kind of intelligence to encourage strangers, arriving in darkness, believing there was but one hotel in the town, and having desired all letters to be

addressed to them there. However, the sailor rose
to the occasion. He was a wizened little man, with
the tentacles of a cuttle fish and the administrative
powers of a Cook.

'But there are many other hotels, mesdames,' he
said, while he attached some ten or twelve *articles de
voyage* to his person. 'Come, I will conduct you to
the best of them.'

My second cousin's portmanteau, ballasted by the
Kodak and the medicine chest, was hanging round his
neck, and gave deadly impetus to his charge through
the dense throng of jabbering peasants that was
slowly squeezing itself up the gangway. But in spite
of the confidence inspired by the sailor, it was in
some anxiety of spirit that we hurried along after
him, in darkness that was only streaked here and
there by the rays of indifferent oil-lamps across a
high-backed wooden bridge, and out on to a long
and pathless tract of grass. Everything had for the
moment a painful resemblance to the landing of
Martin Chuzzlewit and Mark Tapley on the swampy

A PLUNGE INTO THE UNKNOWN—ARRIVAL AT PAUILLAC.

bank of the Mississippi in search of the city of Eden. How did we know what sort of stifling den above a restaurant it would be that the sailor called a hotel? How did we know what *compôtes* of grease and garlic we might have to eat there? We breathed more freely when we were deposited in the narrow hall of a house that had something of the air of a real hotel, and were met by an obsequious *garçon* and a highly-respectable smell of beefsteak. We were shown our room, a palatially large one, with a light paper that would be an excellent background for mosquito-hunting, and we were told that *table d'hôte* was nearly over, but that we could have whatever we wished.

We said, ' *Œufs sur le plat,*' as we always feebly do when in doubt, and descended to a very warm and dinnerish little *salle-à-manger*, full of black-haired fat men, and black bottles of *vin ordinaire*, and pervaded by the satisfaction of those who have dined largely and well.

Much strange talk buzzed round us in the thick Bordelais accent, while we waited for our eggs on the

plate : excited harangues about vintages and grapes,
that bristled with facts so esoteric and so solid that
my cousin said she would fetch the note-book at once,

THE DOG APPROACHED WITH A SLOW POLITENESS.

and slipped away with the graceful bow to the
company that we had observed society at Pauillac
demanded.   I had embarked on the eggs before she

came back, and was thinking how I could best
express the curious flavour of the grease in which
they were cooked, when I heard a slight scuffle at
the door, and saw my cousin dart in with inflated
eyes of terror, followed by a black boar-hound of
about four feet high, on whose back was clinging a
monkey of more than usually human and terrifying
aspect. The dog approached with a slow politeness,
and, as he came, the monkey leaped to and fro from
his back to the tables, the chairs, the handle of the
door, anything in fact within reach of his chain that
presented a surface of a quarter of an inch, with the
swinging bound and rebound of a toy on a piece of
indiarubber. We cowered behind our table, and the
danger was for the time averted by the intervention
of some personal friend of the monkey, who, to
our unspeakable thankfulness, took him out of the
room.

But that night, when we had forgotten the incident
and were going up the dark staircase to our room, my
cousin, who was in the rear, uttered suddenly the

most vulgar, kitchenmaid's shriek I have ever heard, and fled past me in a state bordering on convulsions, with a dark object swinging from the skirt of her dress.

It was the monkey.

CHAPTER IV.

HUTTERS in the Médoc are serious affairs, impregnable barriers that are fastened irrevocably outside the windows, and admit neither air nor light. Neither do they admit mosquitoes; but we had so far seen none such, and we resolved to risk them, and sleep with the windows open. The mosquitoes forbore—perhaps we were caviare to their countrified tastes, or perhaps they missed the usual seasoning of garlic; but the sunshine that flamed in our windows at some six of the Waterbury (I have not mentioned before that my cousin is attached to a Waterbury watch by a leather strap) had no scruples in the matter. To slumber with the Médoc sun full on one's face is an art that takes some learning, and the first angry rift in the delicious sleep that French wool mattresses and spring beds induce was broadened to a wide-awake torture by a series of rasping, whistling screeches from the street below, that made us grind our teeth, and remember every slate pencil that had ever squeaked on a slate. It was a matter that required instant investigation, and it was not a little startling to find a party of stonemasons perched like birds upon a scaffolding exactly opposite our windows, manipulating monster blocks of the creamy stone out of which they build everything in these parts. They were sawing and shaping these symmetrical blocks down in the street as easily as if they were cheese, and in time we became able to bear that iron screech of the saws tearing their way through the gritty stone; indeed, it now lingers in our ears as a memory inseparable from sunshine, blue linen coats, and Pauillac. But the workmen on the scaffolding remained always a difficulty; when we went out on to our private balcony to hang up our sponges, or to throw the tea-leaves into the gutter of an adjacent roof, it was embarrassing to have to lay bare these domestic arrangements to an audience seated, seemingly, in the sky, not fifteen feet away. But they were companionable people, and, if they had not had a habit of walking over chasms on single planks, with blocks of stone two feet square balanced on their heads, we should have got quite fond of them.

When we had finished, with the help of a battalion of flies, our *petit déjeuner* of excellent *café au lait*, admirable butter, and sour bread, we were conducted, at our own request, to the kitchen to interview Madame, having while at breakfast made up from Bellows' Dictionary all the words under the headings of 'vine' and 'grape' with a view to the conversation. Madame was a solid lady, built much on the lines of a cottage loaf, full of years, of good and greasy living, and possessed of an almost excessive repose of manner. She sat immutably in the kitchen window, and kept a frugal eye on the cook and her handful of wood embers, while she directed her houshold and read the *feuilleton* in her five-centimes Bordeaux paper.

All the country was '*en plein vendange,*' she told
us; wherever we went we could see the vintagers, and

MADAME.

if we wished to make a '*jolie petite course à pied*' we

could not do better than walk to the little village of St. Lambert. *En effet*, she herself was *propriétaire*, and it would give her son great pleasure to show us his *cuvier* and all else that we might care to see.

'And peasants?' we said vaguely; 'we want to talk to the peasants.'

Madame looked slightly bewildered.

'*Il y en avait bien assez de ces gens-là!*' she said, with a contempt that we afterwards understood, when we heard she had been a peasant herself. 'I have a peasant of my own; *ces dames* can go and talk to her as much as they wish.'

The broad esplanade was full of sun, and dogs, and sailors, as we debouched upon it with our note-books, sketch-books, and the Kodak, at some nine o'clock of the morning. A steamer was hooting at the wooden pier over which we had crawled in gloomy fatigue the night before; a boat with a big lug-sail was performing wonderful and strange manœuvres of going about with the help of the current; and a full-rigged ship, with a dazzling green hull, was being towed up to Bordeaux by a black and misshapen tug-boat called *Ercule*, the family name of all Bordeaux tug-boats. It seemed to be a market or *fête* day of a minor sort in Pauillac; something connected with a saint, probably, which in Ireland would have meant that every one would have gone to Mass and done no work for the rest of the day; but here every one worked, just as they did on Sunday, and the people who had no work to do went about and enjoyed themselves. We remember once asking a man at home why the people were going to Mass and what holy day it was. He said he didn't rightly know, but he thought the 'Blessed Vargin' was implicated. We did not find out who or what it was that was implicated in the Pauillac *fête*, but we take this opportunity of thanking them for celebrating themselves on our first day in the Médoc. All manner of unexpected things and people went by on their way to the town that straggled on the hill behind the Boulevard de la

Marine. Donkey - carts, waggons, and *charettes*, driven by brown - faced, white - capped women, or boys in flat felt caps of scarlet or blue,—the *berets* that are found up the west of France from Biarritz to Brittany,—a man on stilts, stalking by with

A MÉDOC DOG-CART.

the grave composure of a heron ; and, creeping through the midst of all these, came now and again a long cart drawn by fawn - coloured oxen, who paced with that swinging saunter that became afterwards so familiar to us, their faces and sleek bodies covered absurdly with a thick netted material to keep the flies off, and their neatly-shod hoofs keeping time like clockwork.

We had been told by Madame the way we should go, and we walked in it with alacrity, especially when it involved leaving the white, sandy high - road, and crossing a vineyard, the property of our amiable hostess. It was the first time that we had been let loose on grapes in this fashion, and we fell upon them with an incredulous delight, that was scarcely checked by the hideous discovery made at this period, that the dog and the monkey had followed us. The monkey was chained to the dog's collar,—that was always something,—but it was none the less disturbing to see suddenly, while stooping to cut one of the long blue bunches, the little black face with its blinking eyes looking greedily and cunningly through the leaves, and the nimble clammy claw extended imperiously for the grapes that we were afraid to refuse. They were delicious grapes — small and sweet and 'inconvayniently crowded' with juice, as a certain Irish wood was reputed to be with woodcock, and so tightly packed on their stalks that it was difficult to pick the first one of the bunch. We, however, overcame this difficulty nobly.

Our arrival at the village of St. Lambert was attended with considerable pomp. The procession was headed by the proprietor, who had overtaken us on his tricycle, and now rode very slowly and majestically before us, eating grapes; next came César, the dog, bestridden by the monkey (also eating grapes), and thereby inspiring the most agonising panic in all other dogs along the road; then we came, carrying the Kodak, and bending under bunches of grapes; and after us an enthusiastic body, composed of the infant population of St. Lambert, announcing in clear tones, to all whom it might concern, that 'These'—meaning us —were '*des étrangères.*'

The procession was halted about half way through the straggling village; the tricycle turned up a side street, and the next moment we had our first sight of wine-making.

There was an archway in one of the long white houses, an archway of a shape that we knew very well before we left the Médoc. It was a kind of large window in the wall, about four feet from the ground, with a heap of brown and bare grape stalks outside it, and, looking in, we saw in full swing the working of one of the oldest trades in the world. It must be admitted that we found it startling. In the mouth of the archway was a broad and shallow wooden receptacle, called the *pressoir;* heaped up in it were mounds of grapes, all black and shining, with their splendid indigo bloom gone for ever, and, splashing about amongst them, barefooted, and ankle-deep in the thick magenta juice, were the treaders of the winepress. It was those bare feet, crimsoned with juice, that took our whole attention for the first few minutes. We had been given uncertain warnings as to what we might or might not see, but we had always hoped against

A TREADER OF THE WINEPRESS.

hope for *sabots.* I think the proprietor felt for us — not sympathetically, of course, but compassionately. He hastened to explain that the fermenting process purified everything; the old plan had been for the men to join hands and dance round and round the *pressoir*, trampling the juice out of the grapes, and singing a little sacrificial vintage song, but now nothing like that obtained. All this was very consoling and nice, but it did not in the least mitigate the horror that fate had in store for us.

We had watched the carts unloading the big *douilles* packed with grapes at the mouth of the archway, and had heard, and straightway forgotten, how many *douilles* were yielded by an acre. We had seen with considerable repugnance the wiry and handsome little blue-clad workmen scrub the berries from the stems on the *grillage*, a raised grating that let the bruised grapes fall through, while the stalks remained on the top. We had watched them shovel the grapes in dripping shovelfuls into a small double-handled barrel, which was then snatched up by two of them, who, with it on their shoulders, would trot across the dusty floor of the *cuvier*, up two ladders that leaned side by side against a tall vat, and, having emptied their load into this immense maw, would trot back, and jump into the *pressoir* again. Through all these things we clung to the beautiful, purifying thought of the fermentation, and said to each other that when we ordered our bottle of Grand St. Lambert at our English hotel we should see that we got it, and would think fondly as we drank it of that good, comforting process. At this juncture one of the barefooted and blue-clad workmen approached with a small tumbler in his singularly dirty hand.

'These ladies would like to taste the *moût*,' he observed, dipping the tumbler in a tub half full of the muddy juice that was trickling out of the *pressoir*. He proffered us the tumbler with a bow, and we looked at each other in speechless horror.

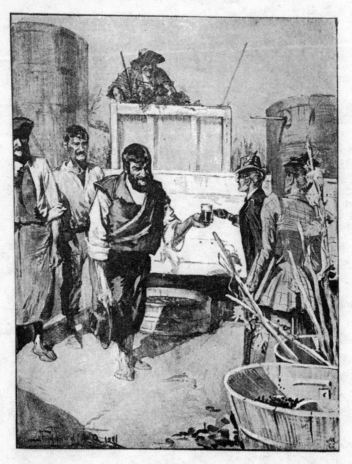

TASTING THE MOÛT.

We were quite certain we should not like to taste
it; but there in front of us was held the tumbler,
with behind it a pair of politely observant black
eyes, and an unbroken flow of commendation in
sing-song Bordelais French. We were assured
that the *moût* was delicious, mild, and sweet, that
the vintagers drank it every day by the gallon,
and, lastly, that it was very wholesome; and we
replied with a ghastly smile that we were not
concerned about its wholesomeness, we did not
contemplate a surfeit just at first; while all the
time we heard the splashing of the feet in the
pressoir, and the quiet trickle of the juice into the
tub. The inevitable moment came, in spite of
temporising, and the glass was put into my hand.
The stuff was a sort of turgid magenta, thick and
greyish, with little bubbles in it, and the quarter
of a teaspoonful that I permitted to ooze between
my lips was deadly, deadly sweet, and had a faint
and dreadful warmth. That I swallowed it shows
partly my good breeding and partly my extreme

desire that my second cousin should not be dis-
couraged.

'*C'est bon? Hein?*' said the *vigneron.* '*Ça vous
fera du bien!*'

He said *bong* and *biang* in the friendly British
way that they pronounce such words in the Médoc.
(We had already found that if we could relax the
strain, and, obeying our native instincts, talk about
vang, and say *combiang*, we should do well with
the Bordelais) I turned to watch the effect on
the other victim, but found that she had retreated
with extraordinary stealth and swiftness to the
far end of the *cuvier*, and, having mounted one of
the ladders that leaned against a giant *cuve*, was
looking down into its pitchy depths. It is one of
the most unamiable traits in my cousin's character
that she has neither enterprise nor good fellowship
about tasting nasty things, and I immediately led
the *vigneron* to the foot of the *cuve* with a fresh
and brimming tumbler of *moût.*

The wood of the great barrel was quite warm,

and from within came a low humming, like a swarm
of bees high up in a chimney. I went up the
second ladder, and looked down into a darkness
that had black gleams in it like a coal-cellar, showing where was the surface of the sweltering mass
of grapes. My cousin hurried into conversation
about it, regardless of the sour, heady smell of
the fermentation, until we heard a voice below
warning us not to stoop so long over the fumes ;
and then I felt that it was quite worth the disgust-
ing flavour of *moût* that still haunted my palate to
see her come down the ladder and find the man
with the tumbler waiting for her at the foot of it.
I could never have believed that she would have
been so lost to all sense of politeness and policy
as to dodge past his extended hand and bolt
through an unknown doorway into a dark room
that had apparently nothing in it except a great
deal of straw and a musty draught.

It was a very long room, so I saw as I followed, lighted principally by an open door at the

6

far end of it, and over half the floor was strewn a thick litter of straw. The open door framed an oblong of glaring white road, and tendrils of vine with the sun shining through their leaves, and the light struck up on the boarded ceiling, and dealt mercifully with the details of a long table with black bottles on it that was disposed beyond the region of the straw.

'It is here that the vintagers eat and sleep,' said the *vigneron*, taking a loving sip from the tumbler for fear it should overflow. '*Mais voilà!*'—with ecstasy—'mademoiselle is about to walk upon one of them! He has drunk too much of the *moût!*'

My cousin was plunging her way through the straw with uncertain strides and without her eyeglasses, so that it must have been a considerable shock to her when a crimson face with a white beard reared itself from the straw at her feet, and stared with a petrified terror at this episode in the dreams induced by *moût*. It was not only at her, however, that the old man thus gazed transfixed.

The monkey had escaped, and was advancing, evidently much exhilarated by the straw, with demoniac leaps and cries, and doubtless the vintager was realising that he must have got 'them' very badly this time. Whatever he may have thought, the monkey settled the question for my cousin. She fled back to us, and when in safety took her gulp of *moût* with a heroism that I well knew to be a refinement of spite.

CHAPTER V.

THE sitting-room in our hotel at Pauillac was discovered and annexed by us on the afternoon of our first day in the Médoc. It was a large room and a pleasant, and, so far as we were aware, had never before been trodden by the foot of man; certainly none trod it once we had taken possession. The sandy bootmarks that we distributed about its polished red floor remained there during the whole of our stay at Pauillac undisturbed by a brush, and unmingled with the footprint of the *négociant en vins*. The two big plaited maize-straw arm-chairs stood at attention by the table just as they were left; and, most wonderful of all, we could open the windows and know they would not be shut the moment our backs were turned. Apparently the other people in the hotel had no time to spend in the sitting-room. The wine merchants went forth in loud companies every morning, but—like the Irish lady who was said to be 'the most thronging woman ever you seen ; sure, she'd go out o' the house twenty times for the once she'd come in '— they never seemed to return, and, whatever may have happened to them, the *salon* remained undisturbedly ours.

It was while sitting at tea at the large admirable table belonging to this room, on the afternoon of our first experience in the *cuviers*, that we became conscious of the eye of the Kodak regarding us from behind our eighteenpenny teapot with a cold reproach. As yet the gardens on the Thames Embankment reigned in lonely beauty in the recesses of the machinery ; nothing French had been given to the mysterious custody of the black box, though we had carried it, at considerable inconvenience, to the *cuvier* of St. Lambert in the morning. The right moment

never seemed to come ; the sun was where it ought
not to be, or we were afraid that the suitable peasant
might be offended, and we had besides a latent dis-
belief in the Kodak's willingness to deal with southern
sunshine and a foreign sky tingling with light.

'It has the surly English turn in it somewhere,' my
cousin had said, with Galway arrogance. But it was
now saying '*Ici on parle Français*' with all the power
of its sunken eye ; and as soon as we had thrown the
tea-leaves out of the window, and hidden the jug of
cold boiled milk behind the stuffed fox on the side-
table, we went down and ordered a wagonette for
the next morning from a livery stable, and felt that
we were going to do our duty seriously by the Kodak.

The weather certainly did its part of the business
to perfection. The sun blazed upon our departure, as
we emerged from the hotel in the morning, and the
heat came through the cool wind in streaks, as the
vanille biscuit intersects the aching monotony of the
lemon ice. Under the awning outside the coffee-room
windows sat Madame, filling out her straw chair in

magnificent meditation. Ours had been the last of the *petits déjeuners*, so that there was no longer any need for her to watch over the expenditure of red embers and *café au lait* in the kitchen, and she could now exhibit her elegant leisure and her blue cloth slippers to the loungers of Pauillac for an hour or so. We wished, for her sake, that the wagonette was larger and had two horses, and that the Kodak's resemblance to a box of 'samples' had not given us so much the effect of commercial travellers; but she gave us a '*bonne promenade*,' and a wave of the hand, that showed she had a heart that did not despise the humble.

Before we had got clear of the town, our *cocher* had begun to betray symptoms of intelligence. Our directions as to where we wished to go had been but vague, and, twisting himself round on his seat, he cross-questioned us until he had grasped the situation. ' These demoiselles wished to see vineyards and vintagers at work in them, *voyons!*'—he twisted up the ends of his little black moustache, and grinned at us with unutterable comprehension, till his fat cheeks must have impeded his vision. 'And they wish to make the *photographie? Eh, bien!* It is I who know where to conduct them. *Allons*, I will make them to see Château Latour!' His black eyes beamed delightedly upon us, and his horse crawled unmolested down the hill, while a series of apparently agreeable ideas displayed themselves on its driver's face. He resumed his usual position on the box, cracked his whip, and frightened the horse into a canter by saying '*Huë!*' in a soprano voice.

It was very satisfactory. We told each other that we had indeed lighted upon a treasure—a man who understood what photography was, and who seemed to know the sort of things we wanted to photograph. We did not know that his mind was occupied in mapping out conveniently those of his friends whom he wished to visit, to photograph, to impress generally with his position of 'Cicero' (as a county Cork paper has classically expressed this office); but we realised all these things afterwards.

We drove for a while through the broad stretches

THE FIRST GROUP OF VENDANGEURS.

of the vineyards, where the myriad low vines stood
with their octopus arms drooping untidily over the
supporting wire, and the grapes hung heavy and ripe,
taking their last look of the sun before their plunge
into the seething night of the *cuves*. No one but the
ardent *négociant en vins* could, we think, call the Médoc
a beautiful land. Even at its gayest and greenest
time these long slopes require all the romance and
richness and mystery of the grapes to give them
an interest, and the much-vaunted fact that the land
was annually worth anything from £250 to £800 per
acre cannot give it the sympathy that lies in an Irish
hillside of furze and rock, whose price is adjusted in
shillings and pence by Sub-Commissioners of the Land
Court.

The vintage had hardly begun. We had to drive
for some distance before we saw the first group of
vendangeurs, standing waist-deep in the vines, snipping
off the bunches and putting them into square wooden
baskets, eating grapes by handfuls, and talking in a
penetrating, incessant gabble that was as strident on

the quiet vineyard slope as were the dazzling white sun-bonnets and kerchiefs and blue blouses in the toneless expanse of green. The Treasure pulled up, informing us that here was a suitable subject for photography, and we docilely got the Kodak into position. The vintagers turned as one man to stare at us, and we tried to isolate some half-dozen in the little focussing mirror, while the Treasure leaped from his box, and, circulating among the crowd, explained to them his position of proprietor of the entertainment with a sense of its humour that was only kept within bounds by the still stronger sense of self-importance. My cousin balanced the Kodak on her arm with all care, and said, '*Maintenant très tranquille, s'il vous plaît!*' to the mirrored half-dozen, who with one accord shrieked with delight, put their arms round each other, did their hair, and otherwise prepared themselves for the ordeal.

'How fortunate it is that they don't object to being photographed!' said my cousin. 'Now, you pull the bobbin—I mean the button—and I will press the other thing.'

There followed a disintegrating click from the heart of the Kodak.

'The photograph is taken,' said my cousin, not as confidently as could have been wished. 'What *did* the book say we were to do next?'

'Put a penny in the slot,' I suggested.

'Idiot!' replied my cousin, searching in my sketching wallet on the earthquake principle—that is, to go at once to the lowest depths, and then to burst upwards and outwards through all resisting elements. '*Here* is the book! It says we are now to turn this handle and replace the cap.'

The handle was turned, and it was then discovered that the cap was irretrievably lost. It was not on the floor of the wagonette, it was not in our pockets, it was not in the hood of my cousin's cloak, or in her hand, or anywhere that it might reasonably have been. We said that we would hold a hat over the thing instead, and on going to the front for this purpose I became aware that the black cap was nestling in its usual place in front of the lens. It was one of the bitterest points of the incident that at this moment the group at whom the Kodak's sightless eye had been directed, advanced upon us to see results, doubtless expecting that each of its six members would receive on the spot a picture on glass with a brass frame.

It was so surpassingly difficult to explain the accident and the general peculiarities of the Kodak, and the disappointment and scorn were so unconcealed when the faltering photographers finally made themselves understood, that as a possible, though doubtful method of consolation, I plunged among the vines and began a pencil sketch of the disappointed ones. In an instant the *cocher* was at my shoulder, summoning all the others with a wave of his hand to come and see the show. It is scarcely necessary to add that they came, and for the next five minutes I and my models were the centre of a hollow square, which was, so to speak, lined and canopied with billowy vapours of garlic.

The sketch was finished with unexampled speed, and in the teeth of the most scathing criticism, the critics showing an artistic intelligence that was almost unearthly, and for which an experience of the Irish peasant was no sort of preparation. I broke my way forth from the square, amidst shrill bursts of laughter and shrieks of '*Ciel!   Que je suis vilaine!*' '*Mais regarde moi un peu le chateau de Jeanne!*' '*Eh! Dieu!   C'est pas moi ça!   Ouf!   C'est vilaine!*' and, having collected my cousin from red-handed gluttony in the background, we succeeded in driving away in time to prevent the sketch-book being torn bodily out of my hand.

We ventured after a few minutes to ask the Treasure where he was now taking us, and after a long and meditative grin at each of us in turn, he condescended to tell us that we were going to see the vintagers at their dinner. Almost as he spoke we whirled in at the gate of a big yard, and saw, under a penthouse at the end of it, a kind of school feast going on : rows of tables covered with platters and jugs, and rows of vintagers devouring untold quantities of vintage soup. Our *cocher* drove straight up to these, and, having whirled showily round, drew up with the air of Napoleon confronting his army, and addressed the meeting. As he progressed with his explanation of our mission we gloomily produced the Kodak, and waited for the outward rush of those who wished to be immortalised : we were becoming alive to the fact that the Médoc peasant had not that shrinking from publicity that we had believed. But providentially the succulent soup, with the meat and cabbage and bread floating in it, was too good to be left in a hurry, and at the end of our driver's address one candidate only came forward, an extremely plump young lady, with an expression of placid self-contentment, and an apron of an infuriated Scotch plaid. The Treasure leaped from his box like an antelope, and, leading her forth to a convenient spot, proceeded to pose her according to his own ideas. After a few experimental positions the inspiration came, and we had the privilege of focussing the fair *vendangeuse,* standing

THE TREASURE WAS POSED BESIDE HER, WITH HIS FAT ARM ROUND HER NECK.

placidly heedless of the fact that the Treasure, with his moustache twisted up to his eyes, from the very extremity of gallantry, was posed beside her, with his fat arm round her neck. Thus they were photographed, and as the words '*C'est fait*' were uttered, the Treasure's hat was raised with a flourish, and a ponderous kiss was deposited upon the cheek of beauty. There was a roar of delight from the luncheon party under the penthouse; even the photographers so far forgot themselves as to titter sympathetically, and as our *cocher* whipped up his horse, and swung out of the yard on two wheels, he turned to us and winked with an intimacy that made my cousin take out her most unbecoming pair of spectacles and put them on, in order to sustain the character of the expedition.

After this the events of the day became blended into a monotony of hot green vineyards, with pink and white houses on the hazy horizon; narrow roads, without a fence between their warm yellow gravel and the yellow gravel in which the vines grow; gangs of vintagers stooping among the plants ; fawn-coloured oxen pacing at ease with their loads ; the clack and twang of Bordelais tongues ; and, most prominent of

FAWN-COLOURED OXEN.

all ingredients, the heat and the Kodak.   Every friend of the *cocher* was found and photographed, the sketch-book was utilised for those who insisted on an immediate result, and, as the afternoon sun began to drop towards the western uplands, we hoped that we might, in the fulness of time, be permitted to go home. But the Treasure had yet another friend, one who lived still farther away from Pauillac, and it was not till we had driven for half an hour that we saw in front of us the now familiar *chai*, with its arched opening into the *cuvier*, and its magenta-legged proprietor standing inside in the juice, shovel in hand. It was becoming too late in the day for the Kodak, and the *cocher* desired that a sketch should be made of this most particular friend, and also of the friend's wife, whom, in the twinkling of an eye, he had fetched from her house and placed on the edge of the *pressoir* in utter absurdity and incongruity. But the artist was too completely subjugated to remonstrate ; even when the sketch-book was snatched from her by the *cocher* and deposited in the vinous fingers of the grape treader with long and loud explanation of every page, she merely sank back in voiceless despair.

We heard without interest or emotion that we were

to be driven home by a different and longer way. Our only articulate longing was for tea, but that being a mere vision, as impossible as beautiful, we gradually took refuge in fatalism, telling ourselves that if we got home that night, well and good; if not, we could sleep in the wagonette, waking up obediently at intervals to make moonlight sketches of such of the *cocher's* friends as he chose to summon from their beds for the purpose. We were in the act of dividing our last gingerbread, while the cool breath of the Médoc evening gave us its first nip, and the vines became fragrant in the dew, and the chorus of *cigales* in the roadside grass sounded like the rhythmic reeling of line off innumerable trout-rods, when I was thrown violently against my cousin by the collapse of the wagonette on one side, and after an instant of extreme anxiety and discomfort, we found ourselves rolled out in a heap into the vines, with the *cigales'* note at our very ears, and the hind wheel of the wagonette finding a bed for itself in the shallow ditch beside us.

THE COCHER MADE LIGHT OF IT.

CHAPTER VI.

E stood side by side, my cousin and I, and viewed the disaster with the gloomy, helpless ignorance of jurymen at a coroner's inquest, and the mirage of tea that had risen before our thirsty eyes a few moments before, sank into the yellow sand in which wallowed our broken-winged wagonette.

The *cocher* made light of it. There was a blacksmith quite close—*en effet*, a cousin of his own, and a man of great intelligence, and all would be arranged in a little quarter of an hour. My cousin with some trouble disinterred the Waterbury—she was in the habit of saying that she had no wish to display it as jewellery, but it seemed to me she might have struck a mean between a châtelaine or a wristlet, and a lair so profoundly situated that I hesitated to ask her the

hour unless I knew she was going to bed. It was
half-past six o'clock; the blacksmith, however intelligent, could not come without being fetched, the
re-fixing of the wheel would take some time, getting
back to Pauillac would take some more, and the
evening was becoming chilly, as October evenings even
in the Médoc have a knack of doing. Our driver
had by this time untackled the tired white horse, and
we were all pacing along toward nothing more
definite than the setting sun, while hunger and ill-
temper ran neck and neck in our bosoms. The road
stretched implacably on to the horizon, its yellow
reaches turning grey as the warmth slowly went out
of the sky; the vintagers had all gone home to their
dinners, and there was nothing moving except the
topsails of a ship that glided spectrally along behind
the shoulder of a low hill on our left, and told us of
the nearness of the great river highway where the
steamers and sailing vessels were going on their way,
sublimely independent of such things as linch-pins or
table d'hôte at Pauillac.

Two stone pillars, a small clump of trees, and a railed-in track connecting these, broke at length the blue-green monotony of the vines; and a low gate, with a little black-pinafored girl sitting on it, seemed to suggest a house somewhere near. It also suggested a possibility of repose till such time as the carriage should be repaired, and we stopped the *cocher* and his flow of conversation to ask if there was a house *là-bas*. Perfectly, there was a house. Did he think its proprietor would permit us to rest there till, etc. etc.? Perfectly, again; in fact, the lady to whom it belonged was yet another of his cousins, a person altogether charming, Madame Suzanne Marcault, and behold one of her children. The little girl was here imported into the conversation, and after some interchange of patois, we found ourselves following the black pinafore up the narrow lane, to demand hospitality from Madame Marcault in the name of M. Joseph Blossier.

It had become almost dark, and presently the last of the light was lost under a thick trellis of vines;

then our noses were smitten by a smell of almost painful deliciousness, and our small guide, who had demurely stepped along in front of us, suddenly ran round the corner of a wall that half closed the end of the lane, and we heard ourselves announced—

'*Maman! V'là deux Anglaises!*'

We followed upon the heels of this introduction, and found ourselves at the wide-open door of a cottage kitchen, wherein a broad-backed peasant woman was stacking logs on a blazing wood fire, and was thereby stimulating a couple of cauldrons to a state of bubbling perfumed ecstasy. This was Madame Suzanne Marcault.

We decided afterwards that we had never met any one with quite such good manners as Madame Suzanne. Hers was one of the many *cuisines de vendanges*, and we had stumbled in upon her at the critical moment known to the Irish cook as 'dishing-in the dinner,' but not for a second did she let us realise how intensely inconvenient our visit must have been. Her politeness was as sincere as the

smell of her *potage*, and the fulness of her sympathy
as we recounted our adventure was not in the least

SUZANNE.

daunted by the fact that my cousin alternately referred

to the wheel as the *boue* or the *rue*. Her heart was
so kind that she felt what we meant.

While we were still labouring with our story,
wheels were heard on the road, and a whip
exploded into a coruscation of crackings at the
door.

'*Ah, Dieu! Les voilà pour le dîner! Dépêche-
toi, voyons!*' A long row of quaint brown and
yellow earthen vessels was set out on a table along
one wall of the kitchen; there must have been two or
three dozen of them, but in a few whirling minutes
our hostess and the little girl had not only filled them
with the savoury contents of the cauldrons, but had
somehow or other stacked them all in the gig that
had just driven up to the door.

'*Nous n'avons pas du monde ce soir,*' explained
Madame Suzanne, when she had ladled out the last
potful of soup, and had settled down into a sort of
steaming tranquillity. '*Ils sont tous là-bas, près St.
Estéphe.*' 'They' meant the vintagers to whom she
was temporary cook, and while the wheels, or rather

the wheel, of our chariot still tarried, we fell into discourse with her about them.

'*Le patron* feeds them well, *pardi*,' she said. '*Tiens*, would *ces dames* like to taste the *soupe de vendange?*'

We tasted it, and it was perhaps the noble flavour of that vintage soup that inspired the scheme that simultaneously occurred to us both. Should we ask this nice woman, with her Irish friendliness, and her sympathetic comprehension of bad French, and her excellent cookery, to put us up for the night? We discussed it hurriedly between scalding, inelegant mouthfuls of soup, sopped bread, and tresses of cabbage, interspersed with flatteries on its quality. We wanted to see the *Médoc au fond*,—what more than this could show us its nethermost profundities? If we had lived out a night in a Connemara cottage, could we not stand one in a French *ferme?* So clean, so convenient, so glowing with local colour. Was it not almost a duty to accept such an opportunity?

It is a useful thing to be pronounced eccentricities.

As we diffidently unfolded the suggestion to Suzanne, she put her hands on her hips and smiled at us with that smile of lenient amusement with which our sojourn in the Médoc was making us familiar. It was droll, *pardi !* She had never before had *pension-naires*, but she had once been servant in a hotel, and if we feared the long drive in the cold—this was how we had put it—she would know how to make us comfortable. *Voyons !*

Delightful creature ! so practical, so unconventional, so Irish in fact, we said to each other, as we listened to her explaining our scheme, with bursts of laughter, to M. Joseph Blossier, who had come to tell us that the carriage would be ready *tout-à-l'heure.* We had left her to deal with him ; he required a more masterful treatment than our French would rise to, and it was with sincere thankfulness that we finally saw him depart, with promises to return for us in the morning with sundry essentials enumerated in a note to Léonie, our *femme de chambre.*

We sat hungrily in a corner of the kitchen while

the little girl spread a surprisingly clean cloth on the table, and Madame Suzanne stirred the *ragoût*, and delicately added to it some further finishings which we trusted were not garlic. The yellowish walls and the smoke-stained wooden ceiling took the firelight with warm good fellowship; the blue china-tiled stove, hard-working *aide-de-camp* to the big open fireplace, sent an upward glow from its red charcoal upon the glittering array of pots and pans and glazed earthen vessels upon the wall above it; and round the open door the vine leaves and bunches of grapes were emphasised theatrically by the firelight, and the last light of the evening and the whirring of the *cigales* came strangely through them from without. The master of the house was late, and feeling, no doubt, like other hostesses, that the interval before dinner required alleviation, Madame Suzanne offered to show us over the rest of her house.

She began paradoxically by leading us out of it, and then took her way round the corner of the house under the grape trellis. She stopped at what was

8

apparently a coach-house door, and after some differ-
ence of opinion between a large key and its keyhole,
pushed it open. A blast of cold air nearly extin-
guished the flame of the little chimneyless lamp that
she carried, as we followed her into a lofty barn, with
giant barrels looming round its walls, and permeated
with the sour, unforgetable, indescribable smell of a
Médoc *cuvier*. This place was about forty feet long,
and at the end of it we dimly descried a ladder, with
a hand-rail, mounting to a door high up in the wall.
Towards this we incredulously followed our hostess,
and having stumbled up it after her, found ourselves
in a musty loft; and then, saying something, whose
import we did not quite catch, about her eldest
daughter, Suzanne unlocked another door, and told
us that this was where we were to sleep. Our
courage receded to the toes of our boots; were we to
share the room with that eldest daughter, or could it
be that we were to join in an even more general
family party? It was a long bare room, with nothing
in it except a very large bed, swathed and canopied

all over with heavy brown draperies, a chair, and a small table in the middle of the room, on which was a toy piano, a manual of devotion, and a little mirror made of something resembling tinfoil.

'It seems we need not have sent for our washing-gear,' observed my cousin. 'I wish we were well out of this.'

'It is a pretty bed, *hein ?*' said the amiable Suzanne, thumping the awful brown swaddlings of our couch. 'And you need fear nothing; my husband and I and *la petite* sleep in there.' She pointed to another door. 'If you are ill, anything, you have but to knock '—

'And mademoiselle, *votre fille aînée ?*' we faltered.

Ouf ! We need not trouble ourselves about her. It was but last week that she had had a fever in that very bed—a fever scarcely worth mentioning; but she was now in Bordeaux for change of air : '*et maintenant, mes demoiselles, descendons !*'

We did not dare to inquire further as to

Mademoiselle Marcault's fever, but we felt that it gave
the finishing touch of horror to those dusky draperies.
It was too late now, however, to draw back, and, expressing a lying satisfaction in all that we had seen, we
followed our hostess's devious course to the kitchen.
M. Marcault was there with another man, who, it was
explained, was a friend who had come to dine.   Both
were dressed in blue linen blouses, and were of the
sharp-nosed, long-moustached type common in Médoc
and both rose and bowed solemnly as Madame
Suzanne introduced us.

'*Deux demoiselles Irlandaises,*' she explained, with
an up-and-down flourish of the lamp, in order that no
details of the appearance of the maniacs might be
lost, 'who are anxious to become acquainted with an
intérieur paysan.'   At this juncture we were far more
anxious that *la nourriture paysanne* should become
acquainted with our interior, but we made reply in
fitting terms, and beguiled the remaining interval
before dinner with political conversation.   We always
found it advisable in France to announce our true

nationality as soon as convenient. We found ourselves at once on a different and more friendly footing, and talk had a pleasant tendency to drift into confidential calumny of our mutual neighbour, perfidious Albion, and all things ran smoother and more gaily. Dinner was ready at last, and we all sat down very close to each other round the narrow table. Suzanne fetched the soup and the *ragoût* off the stove, and helped us all out of the .pot. Our glasses were filled with excellent *ordinaire*, and we began to think it was a charming party. The two men were most agreeable and instructive, talking with astonishing ease and well - bred self - possession on any subject that was started, and giving us much useful information on the subject of vines and vine-growing.

We were most careful to copy our hosts in all things. We put salt in our soup with the blades of our knives ; we absorbed the rich sauce of our delicious *ragoût* with pieces of bread, being indeed pressed to do so by M. Marcault ; we cleaned our knives on rinds of leathery crust; in fact, we conformed, as we thought, admirably. Everything was going on velvet, when, after the *ragoût*, the smell of fried oil became apparent, and from a covered-in pan Suzanne helped us each to a large piece of something that resembled sweetbread, and cut rather like a tough custard pudding. It was fried bright brown, but the inside was yellowish white, and the whole thing was swimming in hot oil. We asked nervously what it was.

' *Mais, mangez le donc,*' responded Suzanne, as she reversed the frying-pan to let the last drops of oil run on to our plates. ' *C'est biang bong! C'est du cèpe — du champignong, vous savez,*' seeing that we did not seem much enlightened. Here was local colour with a vengeance! There rose before us in a moment the brown, contorted visages of *La Famille Empoisonnée* among the mummies of St. Michel, and the dusty bits of fungus that they still retained in their jaws. The situation, however, did not admit of retreat. And we attempted none. The mushroom, or fungus, whatever it was, had a dreadful taste, as though rotten leaves and a rusty knife had been fried together in fat. Moreover, it was patent to the meanest intelligence that, whatever its taste might be, no digestion save that of a native or an ostrich could hope to compete with it. We each swallowed two lumps of it whole, and then my cousin looked wanly at me and said, 'One more, and I shall be sick.'

It was hard and humiliating to explain that we both disliked and feared this crowning treat of a Médoc repast, but we did it; and though we sank in Suzanne's estimation, it was more in pity than in anger that she removed the horror from before us, and replaced it with a delicious *compôte* of pears of her own making. We spent an agreeable evening, in conversation so instructive that we fear to reproduce it here, mingled with confidences as to Suzanne's winter clothes, and criticisms of the sketch I was making of *la petite*. Ten o'clock struck, and Madame Suzanne gave a final tidying-up to her kitchen, and then, opening the great chestnut wood wardrobe that stood near the door, she selected from its layers of coarse brownish linen a pair of sheets, clammy with damp and cleanliness, and led the way once more to our barn.

It was a curious feeling when, after we had helped our hostess to make our bed, and said our good-nights, we found ourselves alone in the depths of peasant France without so much as a toothbrush to remind us of our connection with British effeteness, while the huge empty *cuves* in the barn beneath us roared and sang like organ-pipes in the rising wind. Under ordinary circumstances I do not think we should have survived the dampness of those sheets, but they were not given a fair chance. That night in the Widow Joyce's cabin in Connemara was recalled to us by many things,—things that, though small in themselves, recurred with a persistence quite dispro-portioned to their bulk,—and often, while the mosquitoes piped their drinking-songs beneath the canopy, and the fleas came steeplechasing from the boards to the bed, and the candle burnt lower and lower, and the slaughter waxed grimmer and greater, we said to each

PORTRAIT OF LA PETITE.

121

other that the exercise would at least save us from pleurisy or rheumatic fever.

It was somewhere during an interval of exhausted sleep that we were aware of Suzanne standing at our bedside and asking us in her strong voice if we would like some coffee or some wine. We sleepily said No, but perhaps, *plus tard*, when our things had come from the hotel, some water. It seemed a very short time before those things made their appearance, but it is obviously impossible to wash one's self in a toy piano— a fact which we explained as gently as possible to *la petite*. She retired, and presently we heard a heavy step on the *cuvier* ladder ; something was set down outside, and, rising, we found a very large garden watering-pot full of ice-cold water, and a very small white basin, sitting side by side on our door-step. They were tedious, and the toy piano was nearly washed away in the flood ; but they sufficed.

CHAPTER VII.

*M*AIS! *vous êtes fraîches comme des roses, mesdemoiselles!'* shouted Suzanne, as her two guests seated themselves at her kitchen table with faces of a pale lavender colour.

'Blue roses,' said my cousin ungraciously, as she rubbed her cheeks to free them from the frozen stiffness produced by the contents of the watering-pot, 'and the coffee is cold,' putting her hand round the thick cup that had just been filled for her. The discontented British croak was happily overwhelmed in Suzanne's loud and abundant conversation on things in general; the sourness of the bread was more or less baffled by plastered layers of pear jam; and when we remembered that the coffee had been waiting for us since seven o'clock and that it was now a quarter to eight, we felt that we were not in a position to complain of its tepidity. Strange that a week in France should have so altered our point of view as to make us feel guilty at not having finished our breakfast at eight o'clock.

As we wound up the meal with several bunches of green and purple grapes, grey with dewy bloom, M. Blossier, with his cigarette and his patronising smile, appeared at the doorway, and as he leaned there, with his hands in his pockets, and his straw hat set crooked on his Astrakhan curls, he informed us that a gentleman had called upon us at the hotel the preceding afternoon, and had left word that he would return this morning, so perhaps it would be well if we gave ourselves the trouble to hasten. We looked at each other, conscious of an effect of failure in the morning's toilet ; the tinfoil looking-glass had slurred over defects that we now saw with a quickened perception. This must be the first-fruit of those letters of introduction that had been written about us, and what untold discredit were we now about to heap on our trusting friends! We flung down the unfinished bunches of grapes, and in less than five minutes we had got through the delicate matter of paying our reckoning, and were saying good-bye to Suzanne. It was unexpected under the circumstances that she should have kissed us, but nevertheless she did so. '*Tiens!*' she cried, as I held out a hand for her to shake, '*il me faut vous donner une bise! Là! et là!*' She gave us each two resounding kisses that, as far as garlic was concerned, were not lacking in that local flavour of which we were amateurs, and for fervour and sincerity equalled those that the Irish nurse bestows upon the objects of her affections.

We drove away from Suzanne's household with real regret. We had found in it an excellent *cuisine* and a perfect hostess—so I remarked to my cousin with the dogmatic solemnity of a tombstone. 'Yes,' she said, 'and we found a perfect host too, but he was a noun of multitude, and we provided the *cuisine.*' She fingered her mosquito bites as she spoke, and we fell to reminiscences of our feeble efforts to

M. BLOSSIER, WITH HIS CIGARETTE, APPEARED AT THE DOORWAY.
127

repulse the linked battalions of fleas and mosquitoes the night before.

Very soon, however, we could think of nothing but the extraordinary heat of the wind that was blowing clouds of red dust over us, setting the white sun-bonnets of the *vendangeuses* flapping, as we drove past them at the best speed to which we could incite M. Blossier, and after an hour of combat with it, we arrived at the hotel with our eyes full of sand, and our hair standing aureole-wise round our faces.

Madame herself came forth to meet us, with a note in her fat hand, and a manner in which some slight admixture of interest, almost of respect, was discernible. We read the note. It was even worse than we had expected ; it was a request couched in admirable English that we would be ready to meet the writer at eleven, and he would then give himself the pleasure of conducting us round the vineyards of the neighbourhood, and would finally have the honour of escorting us to his own *château*, where, he hoped, we would dine. The large commercial face of the hall

9

clock showed that we had just one quarter of an hour before this flight into French society in which to eliminate the traces of an experience that would probably have horrified our host beyond recovery, to cast out the accent that we had acquired with such fatal facility from Suzanne and M. Blossier, and to scour through the all-sufficing pages of Bellows' Dictionary for phrases that should lubricate our efforts at high-class conversation.

It was not pleasant, either in prospect or accomplishment, but we did it. We were even sitting in the *salon* as ladies should, putting on tight gloves, when a landau and pair drove to the door, and we were told by the sympathetically excited Louis that a gentleman wished to see us. In another five minutes we were bowling through Pauillac, with parasols up, conversing in free, untrammelled English with the excessively kind and unselfish person who had given a large slice of valuable time to the toil of taking two ignoramuses to see the innermost secrets and perfections of wine-making. Our host told us, in his well-chosen English, that had here and there the pressure and the staccato that an Anglo-Saxon tongue may weary itself in striving to imitate, that we were to partake of *déjeuner* at a rival Pauillac hotel before going any farther. We did partake.

ONLOOKERS OF THE TRIUMPHAL DEPARTURE FROM PAUILLAC.

From oysters, served with hot sausages, to black coffee and fruit, we went hand in hand with the *menu*, and when we rose to go we felt serene and equal to the occasion.

Again we bowled smoothly along the Promenade de la Marine—a spectacle much enjoyed by the Pauillac *monde*, and, let us hope, imposing in the eyes of Madame and of her *salle-à-manger*, now crowded for *déjeuner*. We were driven into the country, in a direction opposite, we were thankful to observe, to that taken the day before by M. Blossier. Heavens! what would be the consternation of our present host if we were to chance upon one of the *cuviers* or vintage kitchens of yesterday, and a troop of acquaintances was to burst therefrom, demanding copies of their photographs with a terrible intimacy —they might even slap us on the back!—the contingency did not bear thinking of.

But a fate very different from wayside *cuviers* and ragged peasant proprietors was in store for us. A couple of undulating miles brought us in sight of a comfortable-looking white stone villa, flanked by long outhouses, and surrounded by a small and phenomenally brilliant flower garden. The vineyards ran like a smoothly swelling sea round the borders of this island that had been preserved from their inroads; the blinds of the villa were drawn down, and it seemed to look with 'a stony British stare' upon the vintage operations going forward all day under its eyes. Monsieur Z. told us that it had been built in imitation of an English villa by the Baroness de Rothschild, but we did not dare to ask why she should have chosen the square modern type, dear to the heart of the retired solicitor. We asked instead why it should be called Mouton Rothschild, and found that once in the dark ages the whole of this part of the wine country had been given over to sheep, and that consequently the word *mouton* had survived here and there; but why it should be tacked on to the name of a family could not be explained. It would be neither kind or clever to call a newly-built house in the neighbourhood of Limerick, Pig Robinson or Pork Murphy; but in France, Sheep Rothschild is a very different affair, and a name held in uninquiring reverence by the *négociant en vins*.

We left the carriage, and proceeded with all dignity

tò the *cuviers* at the rear of the villa, while the hot
and tawny *vent d'Afrique* blew suffocatingly in our
faces, and covered our white veils with yellow grit,
and turned the most inviting shade to mockery. It
was doubtless of such heat as this that the lady's-
maid remarked to her mistress that it quite 'reminded
'er of 'ell!' But, for all that, we had a kind of glory
in it; it made us feel that we were really abroad, and
that we should be able to bore our friends about the
vent d'Afrique, when we got home, in a manner that
would surprise them. At this juncture we were
halted in front of a palatial building of two storeys,
and following our guide into it, we found ourselves
in the twilight aisles of one of the great fermenting
houses of the Médoc. Right and left stood the huge
barrels on their white stone pedestals, belted monsters,
spick and span in their varnished oak and shining
black hoops, with a snowy background of white-
washed wall to define their generous contour, and a
neat little numbered plate on each to heighten their
resemblance to police constables. This was an *édition*

de luxe of wine-making—at least, so it seemed to us after what we had seen of dingy sheds, wine-stained barrels, and promiscuous rubbish, with magenta legs splashing about in juice, and spilt dregs as a foreground.

We were taken up a corner staircase to the upper floor, and were there received by the superhumanly well-bred and intelligent official who is invariably found in such places; we were also received and closely examined by the swarm of fat wasps that, in the *cuviers*, is fully as invariable, and rather more intelligent. No one seems to object to these wasps and their pertinacity; Monsieur Z. and the manager merely gave a pitying glance in the direction of my cousin, when, in the middle of a most creditable question about the phylloxera, her voice broke into a shriek, and after a few seconds of dervish-like insanity, she brought up from the back of her neck the fragments of a wasp, and hurled them to the floor with a dramatic force that was quite unstudied. The wasps congregated most thickly about an arched opening in the wall, through which a crane poked its long lean arm into the open air, and dangled its chain for the tubs full of grapes that were brought

HER VOICE BROKE INTO A SHRIEK.

underneath it by the oxen. Up came each purple load, already battered and robbed of its bloom by the crushing and packing, with the bloated yellow wasps hanging on to it, and the long arm of the crane swung it round to the *pressoir*, which here was a broad truck on wheels. The method then became of the usual repulsive kind. The grapes were churned from their stalks in a machine, the juice ran in a turgid river round the *pressoir*, and, paddling in this, the bare-legged workmen shovelled the grapes into the *cuves*, whose open maws gaped through trap-doors in the floor. Other men packed the stalks into a machine like a pair of stays; when it was full, the tight-lacing began by means of a handle and cogged wheels, and when it was over, the stalks were taken out dry and attenuated, and flung from a window, with the cheerless prospect of being utilised at some future time as top-dressing for their yet unborn brethren.

When we got into the carriage again we were crammed with information, and a silence as of in-digestion settled upon us as we whirled along the hog-backed vineyard road to Château Lafite. It is not only in wine that Mouton Rothschild is beaten

by its nearest neighbour. In the matter of a *château*,
Lafite scores still more decidedly; of that no one
could have any doubt who saw this old country-
house, with its pointed towers, its terraced gardens
with their ambushed perfumes that took the hot wind
by surprise, its view over the soft country to other
châteaux, and its delightful wood, where grassy walks
wound away into the shadows. After these things,
going to see the *cuviers* and the wine-making was
like beginning again on roast beef after dessert; but
the appetite came in eating. It was Mouton Rothschild over again, only more so; it could not be more
dazzlingly smart than its kinsman, but it was larger;
more outhouses and more imposing, a greater number
of *cuves*, a more ambitious manner of regulating the
temperature. We were truly and genuinely in-
terested, but none the less were we penetrated by a
sense of the gross absurdity of our pose as students
of viticulture, while Monsieur Z. and the manager of
Château Lafite imparted fact upon fact antiphon-
ally and seriously, without a shadow of distrust

of our capabilities. Indeed, in all our vintage experiences we met with this heartfelt devotion to the subject, and this touching belief in our intelligence, and it was both a glory and a humiliation to us.

Enfiladed thus by a cross-fire of what might be called grape-shot, we progressed in fullest importance round the quiet nurseries of the claret for which such an incredible future of dessert-tables is in store, and entered at last the doorway of a long low building. A few steps led downwards to another doorway, where a grave and courteous attendant presented us each with a candle placed in a socket at the end of a long handle, and unlocked a door into profound and pitchy blackness. It was like going to see the mummies at Bordeaux, it was even more like going into the cellar at home to look for rats, and my cousin's skirts were instinctively gathered up and her candle lowered to the ground as the darkness closed its mouth upon us. It was cool and damp, it smelt of must and wine-barrels, and in some way one could feel that it was immense. Our guides turned to the right without hesitation, into a gallery whose walls, from the sandy floor to the vaulted ceiling, were made of bottles of wine. We walked on, and still on, trying to take it in, while on either side the tiers of bottles looked at us out of their partitions with cold uncountable eyes, eye-browed sometimes, or bearded, with a fungus as snowy and delicate as *crêpe lisse*, on which the specks of dew glittered as the candle-light procession passed by.

'There are here a hundred and fifty thousand bottles of claret,' said the manager, with prosaic calm. 'Some of them are a century old. This is the private cellar of Baron de Rothschild.'

'He will not drink it all,' said Monsieur Z.; and we laughed a feeble giggle, whose fatuity told that we had become exhausted receivers.

More and yet more aisles followed, catacombs of silence and black heavy air, but full of the strange life of the wine that lay, biding its time according to its tribe and family, in a 'monotony of

ON EITHER SIDE THE TIERS OF BOTTLES LOOKED AT US OUT OF THEIR
PARTITIONS WITH COLD UNCOUNTABLE EYES.

enchanted pride,' as Ruskin has said about pine trees.

We saw very little more of wine-making, when we got out again into the blustry heat, and crawled back to the carriage, feeling cheaper and more modern than we had done for some time. A new phase of sight-seeing was in store for us, and one with which we were even less fitted to compete. The inner life of a French country-house does not come within the scope of the ordinary tourist ; and when, later in the afternoon, we were led up the curving and creeper-wreathed steps of a *château,* and ushered into an atmosphere of polished floors, still more polished manners, afternoon tea, and a billiard-table, there was only one drawback to perfect enjoyment of the situation. The ladies of the household—there were several of them — did not speak English, and at once that delusive glibness that had been nurtured by talking to Suzanne began to wither in the shadeless glare of drawing-room con-versation.

We shall never know what absurdities we said, or what *bêtises* we committed ; we can only feel satisfied that in a general way we said and did the wrong thing, and we can but 'faintly trust the larger hope' that our kind hosts made due allowance for insular imbecility. Whatever they may have thought of the strangers so unexpectedly brought within their gates, they kept alike their countenances and their counsel; and when the guests had faltered and smirked through their difficult farewells, and hidden their hot faces in the shelter of the landau, they were aware, as they drove away in the clear southern starlight, of two great fragrant bouquets of roses and heliotrope on the seat opposite, the last charming expression of the hospitality of the Médoc.

CHAPTER VIII.

T is a truism, venerable to the verge of dotage, to say that the way not to enjoy travelling is to do it at a rush, spending the days in sight-seeing, and the nights in the train; but this disposition of things has one merit, it keeps the anguish out of farewells. The heart-tendrils have not time to weave themselves round the *concierge*, the chambermaid is still your bitterest foe, the waiter has not yet risen to the position of an unnaturally obliging brother; you are too hurried to discover the full charms of the *armoire à glace* in the bedroom, or the verandah outside the *salon* windows, and you scurry from one hotel to another, unregretful and heart-whole.

But a week—and we were the best part of a week at Pauillac—gives ample time for the forming of those ill-fated foreign friendships which are destined never, as Rossetti says, 'to find an earthly close.' I do not know from how many hotels in various parts of France we have gone forth sorrowing, and asseverating our intention of returning there directly our affairs in Ireland could be wound up so as to permit of our leaving that country for life. To their melancholy number must now be added the Grand Hôtel du Commerce, Pauillac. On the last sad day we had to start early,—a proceeding that is a strain upon the constitution of any hotel,—but never, on our laziest mornings, had we such lavish cans of *eau bouillante*, nor such hot coffee, nor such a foaming jug of freshly boiled milk. Léonie the chambermaid, Louis the *garçon*, Jeanne the cook, all vied with each other in fond efforts to enhance the poignancy of parting ; even the bill, usually a styptic to the tender pain of farewell, was affectingly moderate.

'Black,' the big dog, paced beside us to the curious little vehicle, not unlike a county Cork inside car, that was to take us to the station ; he was bestridden

as usual by the monkey, and in her softened mood
my cousin endured the clammy clutch of 'Bamboo'
upon her finger with scarcely a shudder.   Jeanne's

MY COUSIN ENDURED THE CLAMMY TOUCH OF 'BAMBOO' UPON HER
FINGER WITH SCARCELY A SHUDDER.

little girl had given us a flaming bouquet of scarlet
geraniums and heliotrope; two bunches of grapes

had been pressed upon us by Madame, to sustain us on our journey; and, at the last moment, our friend who had been the first to introduce us to the secrets of wine-making darted forward with a card addressed to the proprietor of a restaurant in Bordeaux, on which that gentleman was prayed to serve to '*ces demoiselles*' a bottle of Grand St. Lambert, '85, at the expense of its original producer. Of course we left vowing to return for the *vendange* next year, and trying to believe that we should be as good as our word. It seemed the only way given to us of marking our sense of their kindness.

We had to wait at the station, seated on our luggage in default of benches, before the train—the tallest we had ever seen—came in, towering over the platformless station after the arrogant fashion of French trains; and having scaled its precipitous sides, and struggled up into what we expected to be its lofty saloons, our hats were knocked over our eyes by the ceiling. We then found that the unusual height of the train was caused by the third-classes being mounted on top, above our more honourable heads, and that, in moving about the carriage, it was safer to go on all-fours.

It was a long hot drive across Bordeaux to the Gare de la Bastide, and it gave a fine sense of freedom to leave all luggage there, and set forth again on foot, unhampered by anything except a small cherished hand-basket. We took the ferry-boat across to the other side of the river—a little strenuous black steamer that fretted and panted across the wide stream like a broken-winded pony trying to bolt. We did not know our way, and asked advice on the subject from as many people as possible, only taking care to wait till our most recent informant was round a corner. I once omitted this precaution in Cork, and while I was blandly putting further inquiries to a postman, an awful voice cried after me—

'I suppose you think I'm a liar!'

A thing that has made me circumspect in such matters ever since.

Our way led through the market—a great iron tent, filled with the most variegated colours, voices, and smells. We roamed through damp, brilliant aisles, with vivid splendours of fruit and flowers mounting high over our heads on either hand; we explored the remarkable collections of birds, beasts, and herbs that were being confidently purchased by the housewives of Bordeaux for family consumption; and, with a bow of recognition to a poisonous barrowload of fungi, we pursued our way into the sunny street wherein was the restaurant which had been indicated to us by our late host. We presented the card entitling us to the bottle of Grand St. Lambert without delay, and it was presently borne in in state by the proprietor himself—a civility obviously owing to the curiosity that was displayed on his red and round-eyed countenance. It was a large bottle, with a beautiful white-and-gold label, and after we had scientifically smelt its bouquet, and slowly absorbed as much as we thought becoming, morally and physically, there was still two-thirds of the bottle left, far too much

either to squander upon the waiter or to finish ourselves. The waiter had left a mound of grapes in
front of us, and had decorously retired; on a buffet
behind us were a number of old newspapers; the
hand-basket was on the floor at our feet; all was as
perfect as if it had occurred in a romance of detective
life. My second cousin stealthily abstracted an
Intransigéant of a responsible age from the buffet,
wrapped up the bottle in its woolly folds, and forced
it diagonally into the basket, while the various
matters it dispossessed were forced, diagonally or
otherwise, into our pockets, so that when I came to
pay the bill, the expeditionary purse lay as deep as
the coins at the base of a public building.

Libourne is only half an hour by train from
Bordeaux,—a chequered half-hour of bursts in and
out of tunnels, and of consequently intermittent
amenities on the part of a resplendently-dressed
newly-married pair, who faced us all the way there,
—and the bridge that spans a placid curve of the
Dordogne, under the town of Libourne, came into

view so unexpectedly that we had hardly time to
gather our things together before the train stopped
in the station. We had been fortunate enough to
have been given an introduction to a gentleman and
his wife who spend each vintage season in their
charming little old-fashioned country-house near
Libourne, and we found that their kindness had even
gone to the length of waiting for us outside the
barrier that in France so relentlessly separates the
travelling public from the rest of mankind. It was
humiliating to discover that Monsieur and Madame
A. (I suppose the time-honoured formula must
again be employed) both spoke English so many
thousand times better than we could speak French,
that our acquaintance with that language became
wholly superfluous; but it was also refreshing. It
was a wonderful thing to feel that we need no more
take thought to our luggage, or to the reproving or
instruction of porters in a foreign tongue. Monsieur
A. had a wholesome belief in female incapacity, and
in an instant we found that we were no longer mere

literary tramps, but had been raised to the serene and almost forgotten position of ladies of quality.

In a very short time we found ourselves being whirled off in a carriage to Quinault, the country-house aforesaid, and were being told all manner of strange things. We had not looked at a newspaper since we left Paris, and it was hard to believe that the most notable figure in Irish politics should have left them for ever, and no echo of such a thing come to us, even in the quiet, far-away vineyards of the Médoc. We were now in the St. Emilion district, and without wishing to insult the Médoc, it must be said that it cannot compare in beauty with the opposite side of the Gironde. There was an air of generous luxuriance about the vines themselves that began to realise for us the vineyards of our more poetical visions. The stunted little shrubs on which we had been forming our eye were no more to be seen. Tall bushes, trained to spread like fans on espaliers, had taken their place, and pictorially, at any rate, there can be no comparison between the two systems. There was a sunset that evening that made the first sight of the St. Emilion vines a thing greatly to be remembered. Quinault is a scientific vineyard, and the charm of colour conferred by the blue-green sulphate of copper that stains all the leaves, is a fine confirmation of the theory that the useful is necessarily the beautiful. These blue-green leaves had turned to a mysterious metallic grey in the evening. light; up the middle aisle came a cart drawn by a big white horse, a scarlet-capped man was standing up in it between the barrels of grapes, his figure showing 'dark against day's golden death;' after it followed a procession of vintagers, women and boys mostly, the yellow light behind them giving to the long row of figures the effect of being a company of saints on an early Italian background; and, last of all, came a little, incredibly bowed woman, who had been vintaging here at Quinault for the last eighty years—La Mère Mémé, the oldest and the most conscientious *vendangeuse* of the district.

'She is always the first at the end of the row,' we

were told, 'and she never leaves a bunch behind her, and she has eighty-seven years; *n'est-ce pas, ma Mère?*'

LA MÈRE MÉMÉ—ALWAYS FIRST AT THE END OF HER ROW.

Mère Mémé admitted the eighty-seven years with an almost bored acquiescence. She had been very old for so long that she was less proud of it than she had

probably been when she was eighty. She sat down
on a barrel, and a sketch of her was made as speedily
as might be, while the sky faded from gold to red,

A SKETCH WAS MADE OF HER AS SPEEDILY AS MIGHT BE.

and the rest of the vintagers slowly tore themselves
from the charms of looking over the sketcher's
shoulder to go to the excellent dinner that was

waiting for them in a long vine-covered barn. Once more we tasted the vintage soup, and smacked our lips, and said, with facetious under-statement of the case, that it was *pas mal*, and once more we prodded at the cauldron of *ragoût*, and felt the hunger of gluttony rise within us as we smelt its rich and composite fragrance. We were connoisseurs in vintage cookery by this time, and had been shown the mysteries of many vintage kitchens, but as the exhibition always took place a long time after tea and a short time before dinner, it never failed to make us regret that we also were not vintagers.

We wandered back to the house through the rose-garden, and though we pretend to no horticultural knowledge, by dint of recognising 'La France's' timid flush, and the orange glow of that poetically-named flower, 'William Allan Richardson,' we took a higher place in the estimation of their proprietor, and were encouraged to adventurous remarks on their culture as practised in Ireland, which, we fear, must have hopelessly degraded the gardeners of that country in the eyes of Monsieur A. It was hard to talk of anything else but roses and fruit at dinner, when the centre of the table was a masterpiece of both one and the other; but we were beginning to feel less restricted now in our choice of subjects. During our last flight into polite society our ideas were to us much as the creatures in the Ark must have been to Noah. Our brains were full of interesting things which we wished to plant out on the world, but when we thrust them forth, they could find no rest for the soles of their feet in the strange sea of French conversation, and they returned to sit lamentably upon the shelf, with all the other agreeable but untranslatable notions.

Now, however, we had not only enlarged our vocabulary, but we had also lost a good deal of the decent diffidence that had at first prompted us to hold our tongues, and we found ourselves conversing gaily, with a hideous disregard of the trammels of verbs and the pitfalls of gender. I had nearly finished my dinner before I realised that in asking

my neighbour to pass *la selle*, I was unreasonably
demanding a saddle, and it was almost dreadful that
that neighbour gave no sign of what he felt, and
merely told me that to eat *du sel* in such quantities
as is my wont was an *habitude Anglaise*. It would
have been consolatory to have been laughed at openly
on such occasions, but I suppose such altruistic
politeness would be beyond the power of most
people ; certainly no one we ever met soared to such
heights, and I am sure we are not capable of it
ourselves.

We had an expedition before us the next day, and
the evening had to be short. However, after dinner
we strolled out into the darkness, mellowed by the
scent of many roses, and went to have a look at the
vendangeuses. The ladies had a dining-room apart
from the gentlemen, and when we looked in at them,
were still sitting over their wine with a fine indiffer-
ence to the charms of general society in the barn.
Mère Mémé, at the end of the long table, with the
lamplight deepening her wrinkles into trenches, and

sinking her eyes into wells of ink, might have been an over-printed engraving of Rembrandt's mother. Gathered round her were three or four hardly less ancient ladies, equally suggestive of Rembrandt's relations, and a long array of dark-haired, white-coifed women and girls were to be seen, more or less dimly in the indifferent light, finishing their jugs of *vin ordinaire*, all talking at the tops of their voices, and all, after the first stare, comporting themselves as if no curious foreign eyes were observing them from the doorway.

The evening closed with one dramatic episode. A long low dark room; at one end a bare table; on one side of it an excited group of women; on the wall behind, a smoky lamp, throwing a lurid light on two resolute-looking men, who stood behind the table on which a swarthy victim lay trembling, held tightly by one, while the other hurriedly divested him of all clothing save a fur boa and two pair of boots.

Madame A. was having her black poodle clipped.

CHAPTER IX.

IT was market day at Libourne. We were aware of that from a very early hour of the morning, as the complaining utterances of every class of rickety waggon and ungreased wheel were wafted in at the windows of our hotel, blended with the solid, carpet-like whacking of donkeys' backs, and the screams of their drivers, all ladies of advanced age and leathern lung power. Monsieur and Madame

A. called for us at nine, and before setting forth on the legitimate expedition allotted to the day, we drove round the market square.

A helpless depression comes over us at the thought of attempting to describe a foreign market-place. It

MARKET PLACE, LIBOURNE.

has been so often done, and from such an exhaustive number of points of view, that there seems nothing in the least original left to be said. I do not suppose that any account of journeyings in France is really perfect without a semi-humorous description of an old woman under a great blue or a great red umbrella. It should be dashed with a pathetic brilliancy, and there should, as a rule, be something smouldering and suggestive of ancient coquetry about the eyes of the old woman. We both felt this, and my cousin ran about feverishly, snapping off Kodak plates in the most extravagant way, but failing to find quite the old lady we wanted.

Another disappointment was the peasant straw hat upon which she had set her heart, such a hat as I had bought in Brittany—conical, broad-brimmed, many-coloured. We shouldered round the sunny, noisy square, finding everything imaginable for sale except straw hats; finally we left the open-air merchants, and in a bonnet shop, whose only claim to romance was its position in the arcades that—like the 'Rows' at Chester—surrounded the square, she bought for twenty sous a hat that might easily have been worn in Bond Street.

We were to be shown St. Emilion this delicious mid-June day,—by the calendar it was about the

8th or 9th of October, but it was evident that there

MY COUSIN RAN ABOUT FEVERISHLY, SNAPPING OFF KODAK PLATES IN
THE MOST EXTRAVAGANT WAY.

was a mistake somewhere,—and the drive to that

small but remarkable town was one of most brilliant
and fragrant pleasantness. We were mounting up
out of the levels about Libourne, rising higher and
higher into the bright morning, till we could see some
of the silver coils of the Dordogne beginning to
reveal themselves, and red-roofed villages broke
through the vines on the slopes below us, giving
unexpected suggestions of Arcadia.

Presently above the coachman's hat a yellow
crocketed spire thrust itself into the blue of the sky ;
there came crowding after it towers and roofs, and
finally a tall crumbling wall, standing quite alone
outside old fortifications, with nothing but the Gothic
window-openings left to show that it had once been
part of a great church. We drove in through a
towered gateway, and over the cobble-stones dear
to the writers of mediæval romance and the makers
of carriage springs, and, squeezing our way along a
street narrow enough to allow us to shake hands
simultaneously with the occupants of the houses on
both sides, we pulled up at the opening of a street

too steep for a carriage. Down this we went on foot, reminded a good deal of Clovelly, and yet glad that it was not Clovelly, but a walled town in the heart of the vineyard country, with a saint and a shrine, and a history as gorgeous as an illuminated missal. Level ground was granted at last to our aching knees, a little plateau where was a shading chestnut tree, a railing, and behind these the unassuming front of an inn,—the Hôtel Dussaut, if our memories are correct, —with its doors opening straight in upon a room where a cleanly-laid table glimmered in the cool obscurity.

As we stood under the chestnut tree a sound as of the beating of eggs rose to us presently from a flagged yard about fifteen feet below our plateau, and, looking over the edge, we had an excellent bird's-eye view of two young ladies engaged respectively in beating a yellow compound with a fork, and in shaking some other yellow compound in a frying-pan over a charcoal fire. One of them wore *pince-nez*, both had early Florentine shocks of hair, and a general appear-

ance of such æsthetic culture that we refused at first
to believe that they were preparing our *déjeuner ;*
and when later we seated ourselves at the table
within the French window, and received from the
hands of the wearer of the *pince-nez* the delicious
omelette that had been cooked in the open air, we

THE ÆSTHETIC DAUGHTER OF THE HOTEL.

felt embarrassed by a sense of the favour conferred.
Our hostesses must, we fear, have been taken at a
slight disadvantage by us ; we felt rather than saw
some want of completeness in their attire during the
first stages of *déjeuner,*—a bareness as to neck, a

skimpiness as to skirt ; but as the meal progressed, so did the toilettes. By the time that we had finished our dish of smelts, with their wonderful wood-sorrel sauce, the wearer of the *pince-nez* was glowing in a scarlet smocked silk jersey; and when the roast chicken was placed on the table, her sister had endued a flowing skirt, and wreathed her throat with some ten or twelve yards of amber beads. We could not swear that the *pince-nez* themselves had been changed, but certainly it was only when dessert was arrived at that we noticed for the first time that they were gold-rimmed, and were attached by a slim gold chain to a brooch of barbaric splendour.

It was a dessert greatly to be remembered that we had at the Hôtel Dussaut : the monster pears and grapes, the rich velvety wine of the district, and finally, the *spécialité* of the town, ordered expressly for us by Monsieur A., the macaroons made at the convent according to an ancient recipe known to the nuns. Certainly the ecclesiastical macaroon transcends the secular variety ; these come in warm and palpitating, still cleaving to the white square of paper on which they had been baked, looking like lumps of yellow foam at the foot of a waterfall, melting in the mouth as foam itself might melt, and suggesting the idea that the conventual life has its alleviations.

A small *salon* opened out of the little verandah room in which our lunch was served, a sitting-room replete with photograph frames, crochet antimacassars, oil paintings, and green velvet furniture, and blocked in one corner by the altogether astonishing circumstances of a bed, whose sumptuous draperies suggested the proscenium of a puppet show. The window looked down into a precipitous street at the back of the hotel, and, craning out, the pointed arch of an old gateway was visible at the top of the hill between the crooked lines of houses, the Porte de la Cadène, so a little old-fashioned guide-book to St. Emilion informed us. There was a long explanation of the name, from which we gathered that it had something to say to the bar that once fastened the gate, but what exactly it was not given to our poor intelligence to discover.

Whenever the guide-book felt that it was becoming unbefittingly lucid, it threw in a few words of patois, or early French in inverted commas, and went full speed ahead again, secure from pursuit. The photographs that thronged the room, like Ruskin's pine trees elsewhere referred to, 'on barren heights and inaccessible ledges, in quiet multitudes,' proved a more attractive study than the guide-book, and we travelled slowly round the collection till we came upon a cabinet-sized head of a young lady with disordered hair, *pince-nez*, a swan-like length of throat, and an evening dress of which only a single row of Valenciennes trimming showed above the lower edge of the photograph. We sat down before it with a gasp, as we recognised in this ethereal being one of our late cooks, and at the same instant Madame A. made the discovery of a dwarf easel on the floor at the foot of the bed, on which a still larger portrait of a lady, in the dress of a Russian princess, with an inscription to the effect that she was Madame Dussaut herself, owner of the hotel, and mother of the two peeresses who had served for us our admirable *déjeuner*. We retired after this, and said that it would be better to go away and see the town before we found out that these people were closely related to the Bourbons, which seemed the next thing to expect.

The streets had the noonday heat and silence about them when we emerged from beneath the chestnut tree, and went downhill to where a lofty yellow cliff towered sheer in the hollow of the town, carrying on its crest the crocketed spire that we had seen lifting its long throat above its retainers like a serene highness, as we drove through the vineyards to St. Emilion. Low down on the cliff, below the reach of the swinging arms of a huge old fig tree that had rooted itself on the verge of the yellow rock, were carvings like the façade of a church, and finally a door disclosed itself, through which we plunged after our guides, much as we had plunged into the private cellar of the Rothschilds. We were in the famous monolith church, hewn and dug in the living cliff by monks,

headed by the industrious St. Emilion, in the eighth
century, and going down a few steps to the level of
the floor, we looked about us in the extremely
moderate light that came through sloping shafts in
the thickness of the cliffs sixty feet above. The fig
tree roots had burrowed through the cliff, and hung
in loops and knots from the roof, intersecting the
cold and dusty streaks of light, and the flicker of
a sun-lit green spray at the mouth of one of the
shafts gave the solitary touch of colour to the sombre
vault. It was a bare, immense place, with two rows
of square pillars of solid rock supporting the arched
roof, black with age, empty of everything save a stone
altar or two, and a few tombs, dead silent, and
abounding in dark hiding-places for rats and bats.
'All this makes you experience I know not what
sentiment of religious terror,' exclaims the guide-
book at this juncture, in discreet rhapsody, having
cantered through a page of architectural French,
that had almost resulted in a case of 'Bellows to
mend' for the owner of that admirable dictionary.

Our sentiments were far from religious after a tour of that church, during which we had seen some hundreds of names, addresses, ages, birthdays, engagements, and other data inscribed in the soft stone by tourists. Only those who have seen the coronation chair in Westminster Abbey gashed with vile initials, could believe the ravages of vulgarity at St. Emilion. The pillars and tombs were fully garnished with these hall marks of the barbarian. That was only to be expected, as even the bones in the tombs had been carried away bit by bit as agreeable souvenirs, but one would have imagined that the altar might have been spared. It was here, however, and on the old bas-relief above the altar, that a gentleman called Merritt had achieved his deadliest triumphs ; we tracked him subsequently through the grotto of St. Emilion and the monastery cloisters, but this was his highest effort, and probably the one that he recounts with most pride to his envious acquaintances. May the milkman and butcher's boy scribble his name upon the imitation granite of his suburban door-posts, and may it be wiped out from the will of his father-in-law!

We went on into a sort of *annexe* of the church, into which they used to shoot people through *oubliettes* when they became superfluous, and thence we scrambled out into the street again, and across to the grotto of St. Emilion. Apparently the saint had not been able to find anything above ground that combined privacy with excruciating discomfort, and accordingly scratched out this rabbit hole a dozen feet below the rest of the community, and lived there in damp and darkness for twenty or thirty years. His furniture was limited. The light of a match showed a bed cut in the wall, with a bolster of the same sympathetic description, a stone block for a table, another for a chair, and a holy well in an alcove. The old woman who had charge of the grotto struck another match, and held it low in the alcove of the sacred well for us to see the dark gleam of the water. It was more like a shallow pool than a well, and the water lay still and perfectly transparent upon its yellow bed. Its ancient nymph scooped up a tumblerful with the assurance that it was the best in the world, and when we had satisfactorily tasted it, she lowered her match and said archly, '*Et les épingles. Regardez les épingles, mesdemoiselles.*'

We regarded as desired, and saw lying at the bottom of the pool a small collection of pins, some old and rusty enough to have fastened up St. Emilion's gown on wet days, others new and glittering. These, it was explained by the old lady with many knowing side-glances at our companions, were a means of fortune-telling peculiar to the sacred well. Gentlemen and ladies who visited it were accustomed to drop two pins into it, and if these fell so as to form a cross, then the thrower would be married before the year was out; this was asseverated with chapter and verse, and the testimony of brides and bridegrooms who had returned there on their honeymoons. I searched silently and secretly in my inner economy for a pin; so, I perceived, did my cousin, but apparently

'ET LES ÉPINGLES, MESDEMOISELLES.'

without better success than I. The chief props of
a declining costume could not be sacrificed to super-

stition, and our fortunes remain undivined to this
day.

There was more, much more, to be seen in St.
Emilion, and we saw some of it. We trust it may
yet be given to us to stay for a clear three days at
the hotel of the Russian princess, and to dawdle in
a trance of idleness up and down the little streets,
unharassed by time, or letter-writing, or newspapers.
As it was, we went slowly and gradually round the
beautiful ruins of a monastery in the upper part of
the town, where the beeches and ashes grew freely
in the nave and side aisles, and spread what shelter
they could over the defenceless shafts and columns.
The remembrance of those still cloisters, with their
leafy sunlight flickering year after year on the worn
flags and the gentle invasions of the grass, is
pleasant in the mind—a possession chief among
many gains of that very white day at St. Emilion.
The bell-foundry working leisurely in the blackened
shell of what had been another monastery was an
episode in perfect keeping with the general religious

calm of the town ; so was the Pilgrim's-Progress kind of landscape that we viewed from a corner of the fortifications—a delectable land, lying wide and rich in the hot afternoon haze. Indeed, had it not been that in a quiet back street we came upon a group of old women who sat knitting at their vine-hung doors, and discussed with shrill and personal directness the intentions of one of the party with regard to her will, we might have thought it was 'within in in heaven we were,' as an Irishman said, with an intensifying wealth of prepositions, in describing a whisky tent.

CHAPTER X.

IT happened to one of us—no matter which —in early youth to have a governess who hailed from the parts about Bordeaux. She was a small rigid lady, with a cast-iron black silk skirt, and an environing squint that extended her jurisdiction round illimitable corners, and up and down stairs at the same time. So, at least, her pupils felt, as they trembled in the glare of that erratic green-brown eye, and quavered the regulation early French to one another, even in the fastnesses of their own rooms. Mademoiselle still holds sway among certain outlying members of our family, and on the eve of our departure for France there came a note in the well-known hand, suggestive of nothing so much as a paper of pins, in which she begged us, if our travels took us near St. B., to present the enclosed introduction at the country-house of Monsieur de Q., whose little daughters had been among '*les plus gentilles de ses élèves.*'

We were not near St. B., unless an hour by train can be called near, and our last afternoon in varied French society had not persuaded us that we were likely to shine in that sphere, but the habit of early years of subjection was too strong for us. We posted the letter of introduction, and when the answer came that Madame de Q. would hope to meet us at the station of St. B. at three o'clock on the day following our visit to St. Emilion, we said

'Kismet,' and tried to shake the Château Lafite dust from our Sunday hats. The journey to St. B. was hot and uneventful, and we spent the time it occupied mainly in the futile amusement of finding out in Bellows' Dictionary words that fate was never destined to bring us into contact with.

Outside the St. B. station we were accosted by one of those nondescript, smug, red-faced servants who are met with only in France, and were conducted by him towards a green alley of plane trees, in whose shade was standing a landau with one somnolent black horse in the shafts. A tall lady advanced to meet us, hook-nosed and handsome, dressed with awe-inspiring smartness, and with a chill perfection of manner that awoke in us a simultaneous longing to run away. She neither spoke nor understood English, so she gave us to understand at once; and another point about which she did not long leave us in doubt was that she would have 'scorned the haction.' Moreover, the monstrous hearse-horse had not shambled more than a mile or so, at a trot that

THE COCHER.
181

was with difficulty maintained by adjurations and
whip-crackings from the coachman, before we began
to make the further discovery that we had already
bored our hostess almost to tears. We cannot be
surprised at it; the penetrating regret that we had
ever started on the expedition would have paralysed
our powers even of English conversation, and Ollen-
dorff's earliest exercise is a thrilling romance when
compared with the remarks that we churned ardu-
ously forth for Madame de Q.'s benefit.

It is true that she gave us no assistance. She
leaned back and answered our questions without an
effort either to appear less *ennuyée* than she was, or
to amplify her replies, while her eyes strayed from
time to time to the novel that lay on the seat beside
her—'Les Confessions de some one or other. Par
la Comtesse Dash,' or some very similar title. She
would not even discuss Mademoiselle, whom we
played as our trump-card early in the game; in
fact, she had never even seen her. Mademoiselle
had been the governess of her stepdaughters, and

had left before Madame's marriage with Monsieur de Q. The old landau rumbled slowly on, up and down hill, with the interminable vineyards on either hand, and occasional hamlets with houses crowded close to the white dusty road. At one of these, brightly-coloured electioneering posters of some local hero seemed to offer something to talk about.

'*Nous avons à Londres,*' said my cousin very slowly and distinctly, breaking what had been a long and nerve - trying silence, '*tant de ces—a—postiches.*'

'*Pardon?*' said Madame, with a certain languid interest ; '*je ne vous ai pas compris, mademoiselle.*'

'*Oh, sur des murs, vous savez,*' said my cousin, wavering a little ; '*des postiches, comme cela,*'—she indicated another orange-coloured placard.

'*Ah!*' Madame smiled very faintly. '*Des affiches, peut-être?*'

Then it occurred to us that a *postiche* was a name for a small pad for the hair, and humiliation almost overbore our usual feeble necessity of laughter.

'NOUS AVONS A LONDRES TANT DE CES—A—POSTICHES.'

After this reverse we relinquished the unequal contest, and fell into a silence, dappled only by occasional topographical inquiries, until, as we turned in at a gateway, Madame de Q. roused herself sufficiently to tell us that we had arrived at her husband's house. We drove through the wide old-fashioned yard, surrounded by ivy-covered brick buildings, and round a gravel sweep to the front of an imposing white stone house. The coachman ceased from his admonishments at a flight of stone steps, the black horse discontinued his advance, and we dismounted with the feeling that whatever might be before us, it could not be worse than what we had just gone through. The steps led up to a long stone-paved verandah, with handsome white columns supporting it, giving it a certain air of classic distinction; pots of bright scarlet geraniums were ranged along the balustrade, and there was a group of chairs and a small table at one end of the verandah. From these, as we ascended the steps, two gentlemen rose and came

forward to meet us. One, a short stout man, unexpectedly attired in a Norfolk jacket and leather
gaiters, with a blind eye, and a strong resemblance
to the late John Bright, was introduced to us by
Madame de Q. as '*Mon mari;*' and the other, a
spotty young man in a high-crowned straw hat,
clicked his heels together, and made a low bow,
while we were informed that he was Madame's
cousin, M. le Vicomte de R. John Bright apologised
for the temporary absence of his daughters, and then
we sat down and began to talk seriously with him
about vines and their culture, while Madame and
her cousin discussed in rapid undertones, and with
suppressed amusement, some topic that our self-
consciousness told us was not unconnected with
ourselves.

A little apart, and turned away from the table,
there stood a thing that looked like a cross between
a sentry-box and a sedan-chair; it was made of
basket-work, and as we prosed sapiently with Monsieur
de Q. of the rival merits of the Malbec, Merlot, and

Cabernet - Sauvignan grapes, we were aware of a curious agitation on its part. It was a little behind us, and the creaking of the wicker-work made us look round quickly — just in time to see, to our amazement, a small round female spring out of the chair and run nimbly through a long glass door into the drawing - room, followed by a waddling, wheezing ball of yellow fur which had been lurking with her in the recesses of the sentry-box.

Monsieur de Q. betrayed no surprise. ' My sister,' he said explanatorily, and then he added in English, ' She is vair shy.'

Madame and her Vicomte took no notice of the episode, and we were addressing ourselves again to our discourse on grapes—the only subject on which Monsieur de Q. seemed to care to talk—when a jingling of glasses was heard, and the red-faced servant appeared, bearing a large tray, which he put down on the table. At the same moment a sort of dog-cart drove up, and two young ladies jumped out of it, without waiting for the servant, who hurried down

to proffer his help. Madame's brow had contracted
beneath her admirably curled and netted fringe, and
we at once knew that we were about to meet *les plus
gentilles* of the pupils of Mademoiselle.

It is superfluous to give our preconceived ideas of
these young ladies, unless, indeed, for the sake of
saying that they reversed them all. They were
dressed in shirts and short skirts and jackets, and
wore thick boots and sailor hats, and their manner
had a cheerful unconcern and want of stiffness that
was as reassuring to us as it was evidently detestable
to their stepmother. One of them addressed herself
promptly to the table, whereon was the tray with
tumblers, two carafes of cold water, a sugar-basin,
and a tall bottle of what we afterwards found to be
rum. The other sat down in the chair vacated by
her father, and began to talk to us in broken English,
that was so immeasurably bad that my cousin, partly
from politeness, partly from some theory of making
herself understood, began to answer her in as near
an imitation of the same lingo as she could arrive at,

speaking loudly and very slowly, and using, as far as possible, words of no more than three letters. In the meantime I watched the movements of the other sister with a fascinated horror. She first put two lumps of sugar in each glass, then about two teaspoonfuls of rum, and then the tumblers were filled with water, and were handed round, along with biscuits, to the company. Through the glass doors into the drawing-room I could see the aunt, waiting, apparently, in hopes that her share would be brought to her; but as this did not occur, she presently crept back, and, with a flying bow to the party, immured herself again in her sedan-chair, with a heavily-sugared tumbler of the same dreadful *eau sucrée au rhum* with which my cousin and I were toying. The sugar rose through the pale liquid in oily curls; the sickly smell of the rum 'curdled under our noses,' as a Cork carman said, in affected reprobation of a glass of whisky. It was as disagreeable a drink as I have ever had to undertake for convivial purposes, not even excepting *moût* or 'fresh' poteen; and as we

slowly sipped our way towards the two half-melted
lumps in the bottom of the tumbler, not even the
vanille biscuits could reconcile us to this too-con-
centrated nectar.   But release from the necessity of
drinking came unexpectedly.   The yellow dog had
returned with his mistress, and, finding the seclusion
of the sentry-box unremunerative, he went round
from chair to chair, staring at the biscuits of the
revellers with filmy, greedy eyes, and when he came
to me, rearing up on his hind legs and clawing
importunately at my dress.   I fed him, being weak-
minded in such matters, and then I tried to pat
his head.   He immediately gave a shrill yelp and
snapped at my hand, and, in the uncontrollable jump
with which I saved my fingers, the remainder of the
rum and water was spilled over my last clean skirt.

A chorus of horror arose.   The pallid face and
weak saucer eyes of the timid aunt appeared furtively
round the straw rim of the chair, and she murmured,
'Mees! Mees!' in tones of faint reproof.   (I had
forgotten to say that as the dog was supposed to be

an English terrier, he was called 'Miss,' a generic term in France for the British dog, irrespective of size or sex.) Madame de Q. and the spotty cousin offered polite condolences; Monsieur de Q. aimed some opprobrious epithets at the offender instead of the kick that he so richly deserved; and Mdlle. Hortense in an instant whirled me out of my chair, through the drawing-room, and into a bedroom, there to take off my own skirt and endue one of hers, while mine was sent to the kitchen to be washed and dried. It took a fair amount of philosophic calm to walk back to the verandah in a full white calico skirt some four inches too short for me, and it was a relief to find that a number of fresh visitors had arrived, and that my entrance was consequently unobserved. Almost immediately afterwards, it was suggested that we should be taken to see the park, and I crouched down the verandah behind the crowd, trying to decrease my height by those uncompromising four inches, and painfully conscious that all the gentlemen of the party had remained behind, and were watching our exit with some interest. 'Now *ces messieurs* are content,' said Mdlle. Rosalie, dropping behind to talk to me. 'They will be able to talk of nothing but the vintage till we return— *ça m'agace!*'

We crossed the yard, and went on past the inevitable *cuvier*, through a garden full of all-coloured dahlias and wall-fruit, and under the arch of a gateway into a wide shrubbery with elm and chestnut trees shading close-shorn expanses of grass, and a serpentine piece of water, on the farther side of which the largest meadow that we had seen in the much-cultivated Médoc stretched away to a pine wood.

'In winter they chase the woodcock there,' remarked Mdlle. Rosalie.

'We chase him also in Ireland,' we said, 'but he is a difficult bird to catch.'

It then transpired that our hostesses were sportswomen, and had shot almost every bird that there was to be shot in their district, from sparrows to quails. '*Nous chassons de race*,' they said ; 'our grandmother was a noted shot in her day.'

We felt an incongruity about a French grandmother being *bon tireur* that was probably derived from a confused belief that the period of grandmothers in France was coincident with the costumes on a Watteau fan ; but the descendants of this sporting lady assured us that it had been, and was, quite *comme il faut* in the Médoc for ladies to shoot, and they further imparted to us in confidence that their stepmother disapproved deeply of their sporting proclivities—a fact that did not take us by surprise. They were altogether a revelation, these Mdlles. de Q., with English manners and tastes, and even clothes, while Great Britain's language and literature were a sealed book to them, except for a few absurd phrases they had picked up at their convent school at Lyons from a '*demoiselle écossaise, je crois, qui s'appelait Haut-Brion.*' We wondered why a Scotch young lady should have been named after one of the classified clarets, and it was only in subsequent conversa-

tion that it transpired that the demoiselle lived in
Dublin and was called O'Brien.

As we wandered back through the beautifully
laid-out grounds, with such tropical plants as are
usually associated with Kew Gardens meeting us on
every hand, we heard how our hostesses loved riding,
and hoped to get an *amazone* made by an English tailor,
and inquiry elucidated the fact that the *amazones* in
which they rode at present were made with long full
skirts, and were generally as absurd as their name.

The party of men whom we had left in the verandah were still seated there when we returned,
Monsieur de Q. looking more than ever like John
Bright as he held forth in eloquent periods on the
treatment of influenza, which, it appeared, was rag-
ing among his vintagers. Madame de Q. had not
accompanied the walking expedition, and had retired,
so her husband informed us, with a bad headache,
the result of driving in the sun. We guiltily
murmured condolences, but as a few minutes later
we all sat down round the polished oak table in the

dining-room, it appeared to us that the party seemed in no way to suffer from the absence of its hostess. Tea was served in a rather peculiar manner. Empty teacups were placed in front of the guests; one sister went round with the teapot, and the other followed with liqueurs and cold boiled milk, while a variety of little cakes and piled-up dishes of fruit circulated in her wake. The tea was hot and bitter with strength; the certain prospect of indigestion depressed us, and unfitted us to cope with the not unreasonable curiosity of the other visitors as to us and our, to them, astonishing mission in the Médoc. We felt that our vocabulary was being tried rather too high, and on the whole we were glad that we had to catch a train back to Libourne at six, and had to decline the hospitable invitation of the daughters of the house to stay to dinner.

While the carriage was coming round, I made haste to change into my own skirt. I have no bump of locality for the interior of strange houses, and when I had left the room in which the change was effected,

I found myself confronted by three doors all equally likely to lead into the hall. I selected the most likely one, and rashly advanced. It was the boudoir of Madame, — Madame who had retired with a bad headache, and was now seated over a bright wood fire, with her yellow-covered book of 'Confessions' in her hand, and a cigarette between her lips. Sympathy for her, thus cornered in her last stronghold, was my first emotion as I fled, but sympathy for myself has been a more lasting feeling as I think how I have established myself in the mind of Madame de Q. as a crowning example of the *gaucherie* and stupidity of *Les Anglais pour rire.*

CHAPTER XI.

AMILIAR ground, but with what a differ-
ence! While the early train from Libourne
neared the Bastide Station at Bordeaux, we
sat serene and languid in our carriage, reading London papers, and talking English politics to Monsieur
A. with an assurance which, we hope, concealed our
ignorance; luggage, cabmen, and porters were remote
appendages of travel, interesting only to Monsieur
A's. servant, a few carriages off. The dog from
whose tail the tin kettle has been newly removed
could hardly feel a more pleasing sense of undress
than did we when we drove out of the yard of the
station and saw our portmanteaus squatting sullenly
side by side on the pavement, and knew that we
should see their detested faces no more till our
journey's end.

Bordeaux itself became a different town under this chaperonage. In the restaurant at which we lunched we were treated as old and distinguished friends, not merely of Monsieur A., but of the proprietor, and shops where we should have been ignored became gushing in their attentions. In the full glow of this borrowed radiance we travelled that afternoon along the sluggish railway line that traverses the Médoc, and saw at intervals, with a sense of old acquaintance, the sails of the ships and the smoke of the steamers on the Gironde appear above the vineyards on our right. We passed Pauillac with almost a pang of recognition. There was the church where we had seen acolytes with short cassocks and long boots with tassels ; there was the road along which the inexorable Blossier had driven us,—Blossier, who now would lick the dust before us could our *cortége* but meet him ; there—most painful thought of all—was my largest sponge, that had been blown out of my bedroom window by the *vent d'Afrique* and never reappeared.

It was half-past three before, at the station of St. Yzans, we clambered down the steep side of the carriage, and up the still steeper side of a smart English omnibus that was waiting for us. Two strong horses took us fast along the level roads, and the soft breeze cooled us as we sat on high and admired the perfect propriety with which Madame A.'s poodle sat erect beside the coachman and looked down with a sovereign severity upon the cur-dogs at the cottage doors. We had driven for seven miles, and the Gironde, from which the railway had strayed to meet the village of St. Yzans, was in sight again, when the horses were pulled up at a neat new gate-lodge; we drove in over a bridge, and bowled up an avenue with vines spreading far on each side, then through a wood, and finally under a high arched gateway up to the door of a long pink *château* with pointed towers at either end. We were shown into a large drawing-room, with windows opening on to an old stone terrace, beyond which were brilliant flower-beds, and, in the distance, a blue strip of river ; afternoon tea of the English kind stood ready, with a pile of letters and papers waiting beside it ; a billiard-room opened on one side, a library on the other, all empty, and luxuriously expectant of our occupation. It was our good fortune to be the guests of Mr. Gilbey at Château Loudenne, and though by a fortune less kind we had been deprived of the presence of our host, he had provided for us the pleasantest of deputies to dispense his hospitalities.

The few days that we spent there with Monsieur and Madame A. were like no other part of our lives, and retained to the last the ease and enjoyment and the pervading sense of welcome that came so soothingly to us that first afternoon. English management and comforts were not made incongruous by the aromatic flavour of French surroundings and the vivid pageant of the vintage ; each accented the other, and retired into the background with unfailing fitness. It was near the end of the vintage when we arrived. The handsome red and white buildings which held the *cuvier*, the long line of stables and farm-buildings, the immense storehouses full of wine and wine barrels, were at their busiest, and on the slopes below the *château* the vintagers were working at top speed to finish by the end of the week. As we walked through the long vineyards by the river, the grapeless rows of vines looked forlorn and elderly, like mothers who have married off their daughters and have no occupation left. It was far more in-spiriting to move farther on, and watch the sight that was now so familiar and yet always so fresh, the women's figures moving waist-high in the green,—the men carrying the heavy *hottes* of fruit on their necks, the overseer with his eight-foot pole pointing fatefully to the bunch of grapes left behind by the careless *vendangeuses*, the hurry and bustle of every-thing, and the creamy oxen stepping slowly and imperturbably through it all, with their seventeen hands of height shrouded in grey draperies to pre-serve them from the flies, sentient apparently of nothing except the driver's voice and the guiding

touch of his stick. There is a stable full of great
English cart-horses at Loudenne, such as had not
been seen in France since the days of Agincourt,
but these descendants of the mediæval warhorse are

FIN DE VENDANGE.

used only for the rougher farm-work; it is said
that the oxen, from their clockwork slowness and
placidity, do not break and injure the vines as a
horse might, and though this is contradicted, and the

days of oxen are said to be numbered in the Médoc, they still pace in couples from vineyard to *cuvier*, setting their hoofs down together with the grave accuracy of a minuet, neither slackening nor straining, whether the two tall tubs on the cart behind them are full or empty.

The clack of conversation died down a little while we stood with Monsieur A. and looked on at the work, but one could feel that it was a seething repression, as of soda-water behind its cork. We felt bound, however, to combat the justice of giving the women less wages than the men on the grounds that they talked more; it seemed to us that no created being could talk in such volumes as the male Médoc peasant, unless it be a Galway beggar, or a Skibbereen fishwoman before the Bench. The next piece of information seemed, from previous observation, more likely. It is calculated that the vintagers on this estate eat during the vintage an amount of grapes equal to a hogshead of claret—a creditable performance for people who are forbidden to eat any, and are under constant strict surveillance. 'We cannot enforce the rule,' said Monsieur A., beckoning to us two girls from the end of a row; 'we can only prove when it is broken. Put out your tongues!'

This direction was to the two grinning *vendangeuses;* and, in response, two large tongues, as purple-black as a parrot's, were presented to us, while the eyes of their owners goggled above them with guilty deprecation and an inextinguishable sense of the absurdity of the situation. They had the full sympathy of the jury, and the judge only held up his hands and laughed too.

It was already late in the day, and sunset and its signal to leave off work came soon. The crowd flocked out of the vines—men, women, and children, talking and laughing with unexhausted zest, and grouping themselves in the sandy cart-track in unerring harmonies of blue and white and grey, flecked here and there with the flash of a red kerchief or cap. The movement towards home gradually assumed the aspect of a religious procession. Headed by the sacrificial oxen and their load of grapes, it passed slowly through the vineyards in the dewy spell of the evening, till, as it moved distantly up the slopes and breasted the afterglow, it seemed that a Samian glade and a temple to Ceres must be its destination. It was the last of the vintage, and the first feeling of coming farewell touched us while we came back among the stripped vines; the metallic whirr of the *cigales* and the loud interjections of the bullfrogs were the only voices left to replace the shrill babble that had penetrated every square yard of the green landscape. A suspicion of frost was in the air, touching the tender evening like a spur, to remind it of the tyranny that was to come, when the vines would shrink to brown skeletons, and the winter day would darken above them to its setting, in the chilly silence of the snow.

Dinner was scarcely over that evening when the scraping of a fiddle and the husky note of a flute were audible in the hall, and as we came into the drawing-room there entered by the other door a group of people who might have come straight out of Arcadia or an Italian opera. In front were the two musicians, playing a gay little tune, while behind them two peasant girls advanced, carrying each an enormous bouquet of flowers, with a party of the vintagers bringing up the rear. The music finished with a flourish, and one of the bearers of the bouquets brought her offering forward and presented it to Monsieur A. with a few eulogistic sentences, followed by the second bearer, who performed the like office for Madame A. How in this position would an English country gentleman have stiffened, stammered, and assumed a galvanic gratification; how his wife would have murmured inane thanks with uneasy condescension; and how totally different in all particulars was the demeanour of Monsieur and Madame A.! Each in turn made a speech of a few sentences, with perfect graciousness, point, and fluency; they even looked as if they thoroughly enjoyed doing it, and we gaped from the background with respectful admiration. The fiddle and flute struck up again, and to their music the deputation withdrew, leaving just enough flavour of garlic behind to blend quaintly with the heliotrope and rose perfumes of the two bouquets.

This ceremonial was the prelude of the dance that celebrated the *fin de vendange*, and a little later we wrapped ourselves in shawls and went out to join in the revels. The room in which the vintagers dine at the Château Loudenne is an extremely large one, with a musicians' gallery running across one end of it—an accessory that showed that dancing was as recognised a part of the programme as dinner. The dance had hardly begun when we came in; a few of the smaller kind were plodding round in a kind of polka with only three steps to the bar, but the men were for the most part grouped near the door, and the ladies lined the benches, calm in the certainty that they were in the minority. We took our seats at the top of the room under the musicians' gallery, prepared to observe with the intelligent interest of the tourist this splash of local colour that good luck had thrown in our way. The music ceased, and there was a pause, during which the men filed into the room and partners were chosen, while an incredible clang of talk filled the air. Presently a hoot from the long horn announced the beginning of the dance, and each man grasped his partner by the waist and led her forth. It was called a *contre-danse*, and by the time that a tune of the most furious friskiness had been played through once, ten or twelve couples were standing, not only ready, but prancing in their impatience to start. The men were mostly small, agile creatures of comparatively tender years; the women, on the contrary, were tall and stout, seemingly of a different race, and not by any means distressingly young. In fact, the pretty girls whom we had picked out as the probable belles of the entertainment were sitting neglected round the room, talking apparently to their fathers and mothers.

As soon, however, as the signal to go had been given, we realised that, in the practical Médoc, 'handsome is that handsome does.' The tall person whom we had lightly compared to a bolster, went away down the room as if there were a spiral spring inside the bolster-case, and her matronly *vis-à-vis* advanced to meet her in a manner only comparable to 'the way the divil went through Athlone, in standing leps,' to quote Sergeant Mulvaney. We watched these gambols in undisturbed enjoyment for about a minute, and then suddenly my cousin was aware of a man standing in front of her, bowing, and silently holding out both hands.

'He wants you to dance with him, and you will have to do it,' whispered Madame A. to her, with unsympathetic ecstasy ; 'it is the custom of the vintage.'

In another moment my cousin was swept into the line of the top couples, and her partner, a pallid, oily youth of Jewish aspect, was whirling her down the room with such a coruscation of capers as would have done credit to a catherine - wheel. What exactly she looked like as, hopelessly conspicuous in her white dress, she floundered, hopped, and jigged through the *mêlée*, time was not given to me to determine. A blue-clad figure was already bowing

'HE WANTS YOU TO DANCE WITH HIM, AND YOU WILL HAVE TO DO IT;
IT IS THE CUSTOM OF THE VINTAGE.'

in front of me, and, as two warm, ungloved hands took mine, the only balm left in Gilead was the sight of Madame A. cleaving the flood of dancers in the arms of a little creature whom I took for a stout child of ten years old, till I subsequently saw his moustache.

The *contre-danse* in which we were thus embroiled stormed on with conversational intervals between the figures for about twenty minutes. It was an inflamed variety of kitchen Lancers, danced with a rhythmic fury, and larded with impromptu flourishes on the part of the gentlemen. We envied the bolster as she bobbed serenely past us, riding the waves of the *contre-danse* like a bottle in a chopping sea, while we were struggling in its depths and trying with slides and springs to overtake its impossible rhythm. A reel at a tenants' dance in Galway, the 'D'Alberts' at a sergeants' ball at the Curragh, the 'barn-dance' on a carpet after dinner on New Year's night,— in all these violent amusements we have competed with a measure of success, but candour compels us to state that our *début* in the *contre-danse* at Château Loudenne was somewhat of a failure. Sorry spectacles as we were by the time its five or six figures were over, we should have been still more dilapidated had it not been for those intervals wherein we were talked to by our respective vinedressers as agreeably, as politely, and with as easy a selection of topics as if they were daily in the habit of discoursing to English ladies. In this connection we may say that not one of these peasants of the most wine-making district in the world owed any of their hilarity to the claret in which they lived, moved, and had their being; in fact, not once during our fortnight in the Médoc did we see any man who had taken more than was good for him.

More and more dances followed, till our legs ached, and the cement floor wore holes in our shoes, and then, as we were preparing to go back to the house, it was said that *ces dames* ought absolutely to see the 'Bignou.' The 'Bignou' sounded like the name of some monster of the middle ages, and might have been the local name for a werewolf for all we knew; but we stayed, nevertheless, and presently saw entering by another door nothing more alarming than four little old women. It was explained to us that the 'Bignou' was an ancient dance, almost obsolete in that part of the country, and that these four were the only worthy exponents of it, and had been actually awakened out of their first sleep to dance it for us. A rough-looking boy was hoisted on to a barrel at the end of the room—a boy who had come all the way from Brittany for the vintage (if, as is highly probable, I did not misunderstand my partner), bringing with him the little wooden instrument upon which he now set up a shrill piping that sounded like a penny whistle with a bluebottle in it. This archaic flute was itself the 'Bignou' from which the dance took its name, and the extraordinary tune which it buzzed forth might have been composed by Tubal Cain. The four old *danseuses*, in their white caps and full black skirts, took their positions in the middle of the room with a prim consciousness of their own importance, and all that we had yet seen was child's play compared with the intricate measure

that followed.   The little figures flew in darting
circles, like flies on a pool, to the mad squeals of the
' Bignou,' their list-shod feet slapping the floor in

THE LITTLE FIGURES FLEW IN DARTING CIRCLES, LIKE FLIES IN A POOL.

absolute accord, and their full skirts and white cap-
strings leaping out behind them in time to each
angular twist of the tune.   As we watched them we

no longer wondered at their age. Steps such as those could not be learned in less than seventy years.

The onlookers stamped and clapped, the 'Bignou' player blew with a possessed frenzy, and the little old women circled tirelessly, like witches on the Brocken. I do not know how long the dance lasted, but as we went back in the darkness to the *château* we felt as if the music had gone to our heads; and when I lay down under my mosquito curtains, the dark figures whirled and swung giddily before me, as if the spirit of the Médoc had been expressed in them as intoxicatingly as in its wine.

CHAPTER XII.

HE lamps were all lighted on the long
bridge over the Garonne ; the lights quivered and

lengthened in the sleek broad ripples; other lights twinkled on the masts and in the rigging of the half-seen shipping, and but for the trams and the traffic all things were as they had been at our midnight arrival in Bordeaux. It was only 6.30 o'clock, but autumn was catching up to us even in the Médoc, robbing us daily of more and more light, and blunting our regret for a portmanteauful of soiled white skirts by impressing the melancholy fact that this year we should have no further need of them. We had said good-bye to the Médoc and its kind people, and our faces were turned for the bleak North.

There were four large dark hours to be disposed of before the departure of the Paris train, and, as we stood in the blue electric glare of the station, the question of what we were going to do with ourselves rose solemnly and awfully before us. Shopping in the dark was intolerable, even if we had known one shop from another, and there had been anything we wanted to buy; the conventional resource of going to see a church was obviously out of the question ; the rather unconventional one of going to see '*La Femme à Papa*' at the big colonnaded theatre was tempting, but would either impose in the future an exhausting burden of secrecy upon us, or would finally overthrow whatever confidence our relations might still retain in our discretion. There remained dinner as an occupation, and, leaving the arid brilliance of the station, we prowled forth along the quays in search of a suitable restaurant. We were ready to endure much for the sake of interest or picturesqueness, but there is neither one nor the other to be found in a room with a sawdusted floor, a block tin bar, and a contiguous billiard-table ; and these features discounted successively the charms of the restaurants of 'The Antilles,' 'The Brazil,' 'The Spain and Portugal,' the 'Hôtel à la Renommée de l'Omelette,' and the 'Café au Bon Diable,' outside all of whose flaring windows we paused and surveyed with exceeding disfavour the company within.

We reached again the long bridge, with the trams

going to and fro upon it like fireflies, and with the power of fulfilling it came the desire for respectable comfort at the Hôtel de Bayonne, where we had lunched with the A.'s on our way to Loudenne. We stopped a tram and confided our wishes to the conductor. His tram did not go there, but we could 'correspond;' it would be quite simple— The end of the explanation was lost in the jerk with which we were hoisted on to the step, and in the blatant braying of the driver's signal-horn as the tram plunged forward again. We began our journey by standing in a throng on the platform of the tram, and though a light rain had begun, the samples of the atmosphere of the interior that from time to time were wafted to us prevented us from being specially grateful when two gorgeous red-and-blue soldiers politely gave us their seats. After ten or fifteen minutes, however, there was no lack of room; the tram, having taken its way through promising thoroughfares, shook itself free of all passengers saving ourselves, and headed for the open country at a round pace. Before the conductor permitted us to part from him it seemed to us that we might have corresponded not only with every other line in Bordeaux, but with our relatives in Galway as well; and when, somewhere in a dark and silent suburb, we changed to the rival tram, there was a further half-hour before we sank exhausted on our chairs in the Hôtel de Bayonne.

The advantages of an introduction were shown in the effusion of the proprietor's greeting, and under the ministrations of Alphonse, the head waiter, we revived. We were late for the ordinary dinner, and for some time the clean, electric-lighted dining-room had us for its only occupants, as we sat in a trance of repose and quietness, while Alphonse, with his decorous hooked nose and clerical black whiskers, gave us his serious and undivided attention. It was not until after the delicious *omelette au rhum* had come in, in its winding-sheet of spectral blue flame, that a party entered and took possession of a table near us. From the unhurried way in which they

ALPHONSE.

came in and seated themselves it was easy to guess that to dine was the only amusement they proposed to themselves for the evening, and as we drank our coffee and watched their dinner through its stately and solid progress, we began to think that there are few greater fallacies than the general belief that the French middle-classes are small eaters as compared with the English. That the shopkeeper-like man and the fuzzy-headed woman were the givers of the feast, and the parents of the frightful and gluttonous child, was apparent from their disparaging criticisms of the soup and their indulgence of their offspring, but it was necessary for the guest to endure from the child a kiss that, as some one says, was also a baptism, for us to feel that she was no relation to it, unless one of the very poorest kind. The whole party, as it went steadily through their *menu* of ten courses, without omitting the nethermost leek in the salad, opened our eyes, as we have said, to the staying qualities of the French appetite, and it was privileged to demonstrate for us that the mysterious

15

little tumblers of water and peppermint that had been brought in with our finger-glasses were for the fell purpose of rinsing out the mouth before proceeding to coffee and liqueurs. It was a solace to us during our long wait at the hotel ; and monsieur's dexterity with the macaroni cheese and his knife, and madame's gesticulations with a bitten peach, were each in their way agreeable and instructive.

The *dame seule* is an unusual feature in French travelling, especially at night, and it seemed to us, while we wandered down the long platform of the Bastide, with twenty minutes to spare, that we could not do better than get into the carriage reserved for ladies only. But one glance into that fastness was enough. A mamma, a white-capped '*nou-nou*,' an underling, an infant, and three children (two of them in tears) were already in possession, and beginning the first of the meals that experience had taught us would continue through the night. The next carriage was empty ; better the maniac or the inebriate, better even the Government cigar—these things were among the possibilities, but we chanced them. They none of them happened. We adopted the tried stratagem of pulling down the blinds and holding the handle from inside, and had the satisfaction of hearing the possible maniacs, drunkards, and smokers of French tobacco remark to each other, after they had tried the handle, that it was either a mail-van or a reserved carriage.

We had hired two pillows at a franc each, according to the convenient custom on the Paris-Orléans railway, and thanks to them, the worst part of the eleven hours was spent in sleep that was just pleasantly conscious of the stops at the stations, and was lulled into blander repose by an occasional muffled squall from the pandemonium next door. At Blois the daylight began, and it was then, in the cold dawn, while the train shuffled uneasily to and fro on meaningless sidings, and the green-grey mass of a great castle deepened each time we looked from behind the blinds, that we drew forth the half bottle of Grand St. Lambert that had for the last few days been carried perilously about in a bonnet-box, and with grapes and *croissants* began a repast that continued through stages of bovril, tea, and ginger-bread biscuits till we neared Paris. The water for the tea was near proving a difficulty. To get it, it was necessary to shuffle in 'night's disarray' to the buffet, and a fair amount of nerve was required to advance through the crowd of sleepily devouring men and fill a disreputable tin kettle from a carafe of water under the very eyes of an indignant waiter. We flatter ourselves that the most courageous man of our acquaintance would have been afraid to do it.

There is on the south side of the Seine, not far from the Gare Montparnasse, a hotel beloved of art students. It is clean and cheap, and is bounded on all sides by the tram lines that cleave Paris through and through, and put the whole town in the hollow of one's hand for six sous (*avec correspondance*). The Quartier Latin looked as fresh and clean and respect-able on this October morning as if it had not a world-wide reputation for opposite qualities, and as

mademoiselle of the hotel rushed out and greeted us
in such strange English as is learnt from American
art students, and with the effusion that is reserved by
her for old friends, a serene assurance settled down
upon us that here, at least, our appearance, manners,
and accents would excite no surprise. We had our
luncheon at a *crêmerie*, a place known of yore, where
a beefsteak (*saignant*, according to French custom,
unless specially forbidden), *confiture*, a saucerful of
curd known as *fromage à la crême*, and a cup of
black coffee could be obtained in sufficient cleanliness for a franc or less. It was rather too early in
the season for the art student to be in full bloom ;
the two hot little rooms that were so like the cabins
of an inferior steamer were almost empty, instead of
being stuffed to their utmost capacity and resounding
with as many languages as the Tower of Babel, and
when we went on to the studio, and, with pleasurable
anticipation, climbed the long staircase and knocked
at the door, no voice responded. There was no one
there. The easels were heaped up in one corner, the

stools in another, the clock had stopped, the model stand was covered with dust, and desponding sketches of undressed deformities dangled from the walls, each by a single drawing-pin.   Angelo, the hoary and picturesque attendant, followed us into this desolation, and said that such *monde* as there was, with a contemptuous shrug, was *là-bas*.   A glance into the lower studio, where half-a-dozen unknown English-women were fighting over the position of a sulky model in the dress of a cardinal, was enough for us. We felt that 'superfluous lags the veteran on the stage.'

We wandered on by familiar ways to the Luxem-bourg galleries—there, at least, we should find old friends ; and we looked at Rosa Bonheur's oxen with the eye of knowledge, and found them by no means up to the standard of Château Loudenne.   When we got out into the gardens again, with their linked battalions of perambulators, and their thousand children courting sea-sickness on the zoological merry-go-rounds, the afternoon was still young.   The tops of the tall horse-chestnuts were yellow in the sunshine, and above them, in the blue sky, the Eiffel Tower looked down on us, suggesting absurdly the elongated neck of Alice in Wonderland, when the pigeon accuses her of being a serpent. Its insistent challenge could no longer be resisted; in spite of the needle-cases, yard-measures, and paper-weights that had horridly familiarised us with its outlines, it was decidedly a thing to be done. People who would go to sleep if we talked to them about the vineyards, would wake to active contempt if they heard we had not been to the Eiffel Tower.

We were deluded into getting off our tram too soon, and consequently had a long crawl through the empty Exhibition buildings and grounds before we reached our destination. To this, however, we owed the sight of the strange row of variety entertainments which we passed *en route*. A cup of coffee at forty-five centimes, or even a glass of beer at thirty centimes, would have entitled us to a chair or a marble table at any of these spectacles; but having taken a cursory

view, from outside the crowd at the barriers, of the
man in evening clothes mournfully bellowing something that sounded like a funeral ode to his mother,
of the young lady with long yellow hair and short
yellow petticoats giving a comic recitation flavoured
with dancing, and of the infant phenomenon, whose
performance on the piano was unfortunately reduced
to dumb show by the success of the funny man next
door, we were disposed to think that the coffee would
be dear at the price.

We found ourselves at last under the four arching
dachshund legs from which the Tower tapers im-
probably into space, and strayed round on the gravel
underneath it, lavishing upon each other truisms
appropriate to the occasion, and expressing artificial
regrets that we had apparently come too late in the
afternoon for the lift. While we spoke, a clicking
sound dropped to us from the sky; we looked up,
and saw amidst the cobwebs of iron a large square
fly descending. I hardly know how we came to find
ourselves at the entrance of the *ascenseur*. We both

dislike lifts; and my cousin can repeat many rousing tales of lift-accidents, in which the point is usually the apparent identity of the attendant with the leading character in a thrice-repeated nightmare; but some form of false shame impelled us to the first stage. We held our breaths as we slid upwards through the girders that looked like all the propositions in Euclid run mad, and it was not till the horrible hiccough came, that told us we had stopped at the first platform, that we ventured to glance at the lift-man.

We walked round the long galleries, my cousin making herself both conspicuous and absurd by her determination to find out how many dragoon-like strides went to each side. It will doubtless be a blow to the designer to hear that the four faces of the Tower vary in length, two of them measuring ninety-seven yards, another a hundred, and the fourth ninety-nine and a hop. We had thought of going to the top—thought of it vaguely and valiantly for some little time after the lift had shaken us out on the first *étage*, and before we had looked over the edge. One glance, however, down at the black specks crawling on the strips of tape that represented the gravel paths of the Exhibition grounds satisfied us that we were as high as we wished to go. Even here the height was making my fingers tingle, and my cousin had retired unsteadily from the verge under the pretext of buying a photograph at a neighbouring stall; while as to the view, all Paris was already far below us, a marvellous gray and green toy, with the afternoon sun striking flame out of the tiny gilded domes and spires, and the pale thread of a river winding from one microscopic bridge to another, all showing clear in the smokeless air with a magical precision of detail.

There is a staircase that circles dizzily down the Tower, a Jacob's ladder that would make an angel giddy, and rather than enter again the lift that was even now sliding down to us on its steel cable through the iron network, my cousin said she would walk down. It was the final dispute of the expedition,

and, after affording much amusement to the by-
standers, it ended in my leading my cousin, with her
eyes tightly shut, and the expression of Lady Jane
Grey on her way to execution, into the box with the
sloping floor, in whose safety it was so impossible to
believe. We sit safely now in the ground floor of a
two-storeyed house, and as we look back to that
experience, it seems to us that no dentist's chair
can have cradled more suffering than the lift of the
Eiffel Tower.

We left Paris by a late train that night. Summer
and its habiliments had alike been crushed out of
sight by dint of a final war-dance upon our portmanteaus. Everything connected with the Médoc
was put away; the Kodak, with its hidden
store of vintage pictures, the apparatus of afternoon tea, even the well-thumbed and invaluable
copy of Bellows' Dictionary that had up to
this abided immutably in our pockets, was laid
sorrowing to rest in the crown of the Libourne
straw hat. What use was it to us on a degraded

line of railway on which all the porters spoke English?

We took a last look out of the train window at the

SUCCESS TO THE VINTAGE OF 1891.

electric star of the Eiffel Tower, perched among the elder stars in the sky behind us, and my cousin opened her bonnet-box and drew forth for the last time that widow's cruse, the bottle of Grand St. Lambert. There was about a wine-glassful left, and out of a thick green Pauillac mug we solemnly drank success to our first vintage.